Edward Hopper 1882-1967

Hayward Gallery, London
11 February to 29 March 1981

A selection from the exhibition
Edward Hopper: The Art and The Artist
held at the Whitney Museum of American Art in New York
from 16 September 1980 to 25 January 1981
and supported by the National Endowment for the Arts
and Philip Morris Incorporated.

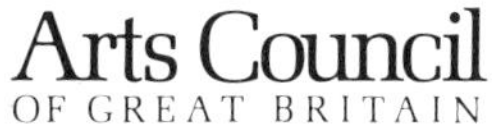

Arts Council Exhibition Officer: Susan Ferleger Brades
assisted by Evie Chondros

Designed by Herbert and Mafalda Spencer
Printed by Gavin Martin Ltd, London
Photographs courtesy of Four Corner Films, London

ISBN 0 7287 0272 X

cover illustration:
drawing for painting, *Nighthawks,* 1942
(cat.no.192)

Note:
Another exhibition, again provided by the Whitney Museum of American Art, *Edward Hopper: The Formative Years,* can be seen at the Newport Museum and Art Gallery (10 January to 14 February), the Fruit Market Gallery, Edinburgh (28 February to 4 April) and the Mostyn Art Gallery, Llandudno (15 August to 3 October). These showings have been arranged by the Welsh and Scottish Arts Councils.

Acknowledgements

It has been the Arts Council's ambition for many years to show the work of Edward Hopper in London. The occasion presented itself when the Whitney Museum of American Art in New York offered a generous selection from the exhibition *Edward Hopper: The Art and The Artist* for a European tour – the London showing precedes others in Amsterdam and Dusseldorf. We are immensely grateful to the Whitney Museum, especially to its Director Tom Armstrong and to Gail Levin, Curator of the Museum's Hopper Collection. Miss Levin selected and arranged the exhibition at the Whitney and was also responsible for the touring selection. The exhibition has been supported by The National Endowment for the Arts and has benefited from sponsorship by Philip Morris Incorporated to whom we are indebted for a grant towards the cost of the Hayward showing.

We would also like to thank Ian Jeffrey for his introduction to our catalogue, and Alfred Kazin and *The New York Times* for permission to reprint an article which first appeared in *The New York Times Magazine* on the occasion of the opening of the Whitney exhibition in September 1980. Mr Jeffrey has asked us to acknowledge his particular debt to Gail Levin's invaluable monograph *Edward Hopper: The Art and The Artist* published for the New York exhibition by W.W.Norton & Company in association with the Whitney Museum of American Art. The poem by Robert Frost is reprinted by kind permission of Jonathan Cape, London.

Joanna Drew
Director of Art

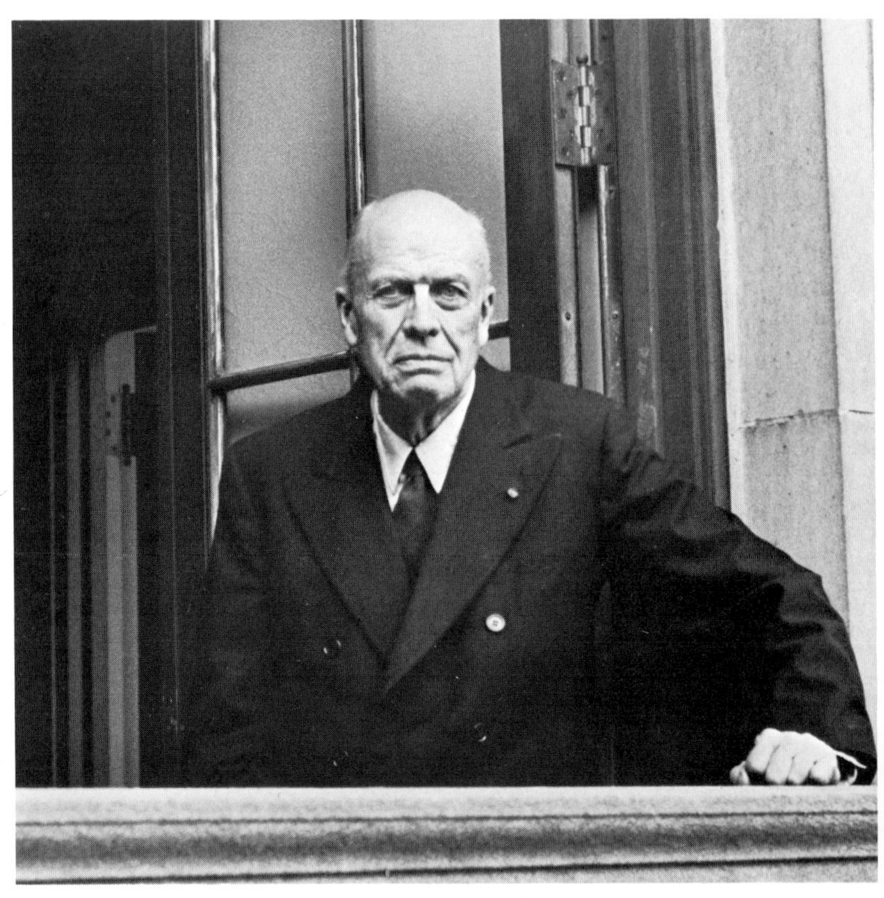

Edward Hopper at the American Academy of Arts
and Letters Ceremonial, 1961
Photograph by Sidney Waintrob of Waintrob/Budd.

A Painter's Strategies

by Ian Jeffrey

Edward Hopper is, in many respects, the most mysterious of all American artists. Much has been read into his works, especially concerning American loneliness and alienation in urban settings, yet he presented himself as an artificer, interested in technical problems: how to reconcile three sources of light in a picture; how to find forms for such uncentred subjects as highways and railroads. He was, and is, generally classified as a realist of sorts, yet he himself thought that 'the realism thing' had been overdone. He wrote, in the '30s, of major painting as a record of the artist's emotions, yet is often judged to be a completely impersonal painter – a camera-eye, quite uninvolved with his subjects.

In fact, Hopper resisted classification, virtually as a matter of policy. In 1927 he envisaged 'the crystallization of the art of America into something native and distinct' and in the '30s critics considered him to be the foremost painter of the American Scene. In 1941, however, he exhibited a number of his early paintings, including 11 French scenes, as though to indicate the diversity of his background. Later he spoke sharply against the 'American Scene' business: 'I always wanted to do myself. The French painters didn't talk about the "French Scene", or the English painters about the "English Scene"'. In his infrequent comments on his own pictures he usually suggested that there was more to them than met the eye: 'You know, there are many thoughts, many impulses that go into a picture' (1960).

Nonetheless, Edward Hopper was an American Scene painter – and that in a quite particular respect. In 1939 he was represented in the large 10th Anniversary Exhibition at the Museum of Modern Art, 'Art In Our Time', by one painting, *House by the Railroad* (1925), and introduced rather as an architectural revivalist than as an artist: 'With Burchfield, helped to make Americans aware of the

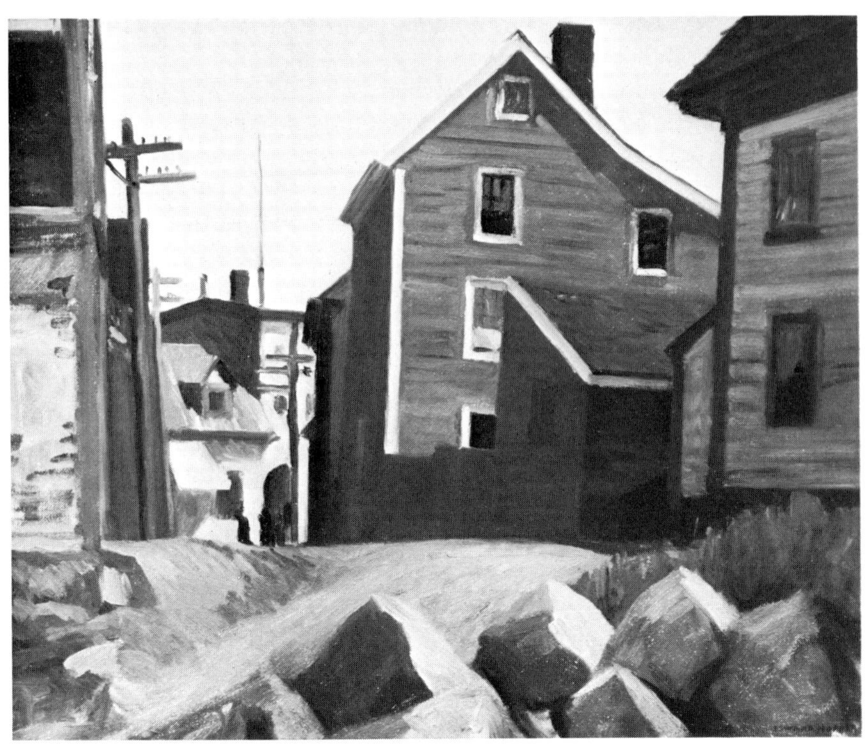

41 · Italian Quarter, Gloucester, 1912

picturesque dignity of late 19th century architecture'. Since 1923 he had been known as a painter of architecture. In that year he sold a watercolour, *The Mansard Roof,* to the Brooklyn Museum for $100 – his first sale of a painting since 1913. This had been painted in the coastal village of Gloucester, Massachusetts, where he and his wife frequently spent their summers in the '20s and early '30s. Much, though not all, of his painting at this time is of unpopulated architecture: *Hodgkin's House, Cape Ann, Massachusetts,* (1928), and *Coast Guard Station* (1929) – both in this exhibition.

Hopper remarked, with characteristic simplicity, that *The Mansard Roof* interested him 'because of the variety of roofs and windows', and added that Mansard roofs had always interested him – like subjects with three distinct sources of light they undoubtedly raised intricate pictorial problems. But architecture provided more than a formal challenge; it was to Hopper, and to other Americans, one of the arts, with drama and literature, which had crystallized into 'something native and distinct' (1927 – in an article on John Sloan, another major American painter who spent time in Gloucester). Thus to paint architecture was to deal with and to question fundamentally American material. Through the expressiveness of buildings it was possible to contact and to understand the original experience of American builders – as Hopper remarked in a later interview regarding his Gloucester work: 'It is a solid looking town. The roofs are very bold, the cornices are bolder. The dormers cast very positive shadows. The sea captain influence I guess – the boldness of ships'.

He was only one of several artists preoccupied by the American past and by native America, but most of his contemporaries celebrated American life and landscape. Thomas Hart Benton brought back animated reports from cotton country and the Louisiana rice fields. Charles Burchfield painted picturesque watercolours of provincial streets. No one else was so attentive to architecture – no one, that is, except photographers. In 1928 Ben Judah Lubschez began work on a photographic survey of the *Plantations of the Carolina Low Country,* eventually completed in 1938 by Frances Benjamin Johnson, and published with a cautionary introduction on the need to keep the past in mind, especially a past which built according to immediate need and local conditions. In 1933 Walker Evans, later to win fame with *American Photographs* (mainly architectural) in 1938, surveyed Victorian buildings in the Boston area for Lincoln Kirstein and the Museum of Modern Art. In 1935 Aaron Siskind set out to document Colonial architecture in Bucks County, Pennsylvania, just as he had documented Carpenter Gothic buildings on Martha's Vineyard the year before.

Of all American artists Walker Evans is the nearest in style and temperament to Hopper. They were both alike interested in architecture. Beyond that both were preoccupied by fabrication. They made pictures as architects made houses, and both delighted in the gauging and crafting of artefacts. Evans, addicted to culture and all its works, boasted that he had never photographed a tree. Hopper, a constant theatre and film-goer, was a devotee of artifice: 'Notice how artificial trees look at night? Trees look like a theatre at night.'

Each worked with a restrictive, even reductive, medium: Evans with monochrome photography, and Hopper with a simplified, planar style, using few colours. Hopper chose to work as he did. Between 1916 and 1919 he spent his summers at Monhegan Island, Maine where he painted the rocky coastline and the sea. His paintings from these years mimic Nature's expressive turbulence. Earlier pictures, such as *Gloucester Harbour* (1912), depict the world with an airy largeness: wind pulls at sails, bends the trees and sends clouds scudding through the skies – as it does time and time again in his French paintings of 1907-9. The same scudding vigour characterises the etchings which he made up to 1923. Prior to that date he was known largely as an illustrator and etcher, but had given most of this work up in favour of painting by 1924 – when his paintings began to find a ready market.

Although the wind still blows through many of his watercolours after 1923 his oil paintings become conspicuously still, like tableaux in which the essence of a moment has been transfixed for perpetuity. Moreover they are increasingly declared as fabrications, as products of a painter's craft. Hopper extends an invitation to his audience to work with him through the means by which he represents. He courts difficulties, spatial difficulties especially, and resolves them less by punctilious accuracy of tone and colour than by a deployment of such devices as a fire hydrant, a barber pole, lamp standards and telegraph poles – all of which cast shadows and in an orderly, calculated way tell us of recession into the picture and of the fall of light.

Early Sunday Morning (1930) is a picture elaborately in this vein. It looks like unpromising terrain for a painter: a screen of commonplace shops on the south-facing side of 7th Avenue, seen in elevation from directly across the street. Hopper indicates depth in a series of darkened doorways, signifies a space in front of the facade by the cast shadows of projecting sign boards, and allows us to gauge the width of the pavement by means of a fire hydrant placed by the kerb and a barber pole close in to a shop front.

Similar markers – lamp posts and telegraph poles – introduce a dipping street in *East Wind Over Weehawken* (1934). In this very intricate picture Hopper has exaggerated the scale of such features as stairways, decorative urns, balustrades and porticos. His two preliminary drawings show these items as unobtrusive details in the ensemble. One result of this overstatement of minutiae in the final version is a maximum of legibility. Every feature chosen for inclusion is stressed and clarified, even to the extent of keeping most of the east-facing windows along the receding street of comparable size. Hopper overcomes this necessary discrepancy by means of marker poles which chart recession, just as the hydrant and barber's sign articulate the even ribbon of pavement in *Early Sunday Morning.* All of which is to say that Hopper is a picture-maker intent on emblematic clarity, and that his use of familiar markers allows him to work unhindered with unbroken planes of colour. Thus he makes images which simultaneously have the clarity of flags, and something of the depth of the world to which they refer.

He admired the Civil War photographs of Mathew Brady and, in an interview with William Johnson, said this of them: 'There was something about the way he took pictures. Someone said it was the lens they had in those days – not sharp. But anyway the pictures aren't cluttered up with detail; you just get what is important. Very simplified.' He might well have been describing his own pictures with their bold features, plain grounds and

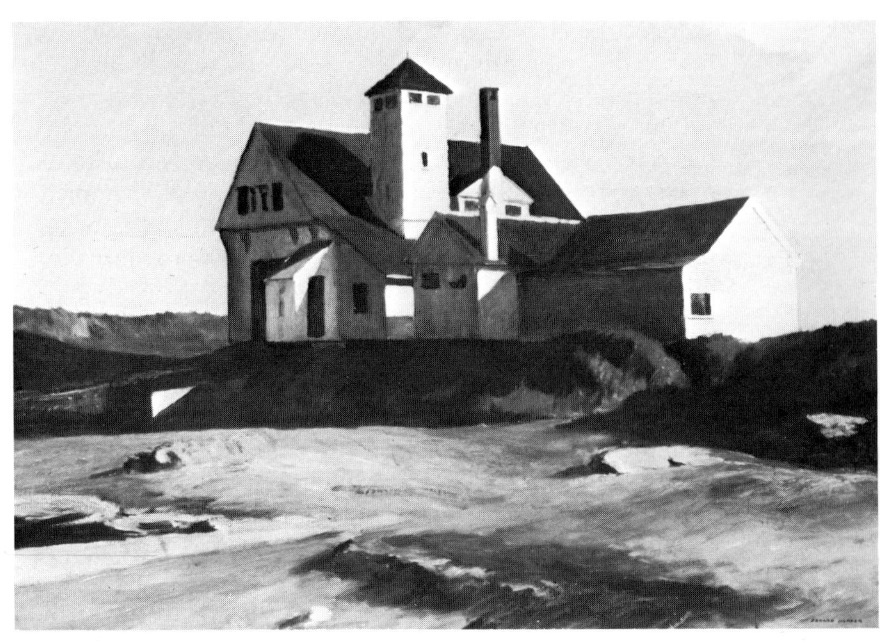

74 · Coast Guard Station, 1929

eschewal of nuanced tonal variations. Yet he did not simplify solely for the sake of immediate legibility. Time and again he clustered like elements together: a range of windows, a sequence of panelling, a cluster of lamps, a flight of steps. His very well-known *New York Movie* (1939) is rich is such groupings: curtains, lamps, coffering, seating. The original drawing for this composition shows a complicated space with many seats and a long flight of steps. In the finished painting the original profusion is reduced; he chooses to deal with sets of threes and fours – limited groupings which invite comparison between near, but marginally dissimilar, neighbours.

This is how he notes particularity, and how he always noted it – especially in townscapes, where his favourite motifs were sets of windows, variously shuttered, canopied and curtained. Walker Evans, among the photographers, honoured particularity in the same way, in symmetrically disposed pictures of facades, doorways and windows – equal halves worn and weathered differently.

Edward Hopper strove to do justice to specifics, to this window with the blinds drawn and to that half-open to catch the breeze. Yet these specifics included more than the tangible elements of the scene in front of him: they included time of day and season, and the feeling of sunlight, wind and water. He had caught these qualities in the briskness of his early painting, when he worked in harmony with the whirl of Nature. In his later, more deliberated pictures, made from the '20s onward, such immaterial qualities were harder to realise, but they continued to preoccupy him. Indeed they continued to be a primary concern, and help account for such puzzling components as the 'lonely' figures who crop up in so many of his paintings.

Some of these, such as the *Girl at a Sewing Machine* (c. 1921), the housekeeper in *Apartment Houses* (1923) and the seated cigar-smoker in *Sunday* (1926), are genre figures and survivors from a realist heyday twenty years before. But the same cannot be said of all Hopper's protagonists, even in the '20s: the passing nun in *New York Pavements* (1924) registers the gusty street, her wind-pulled cowl like a displaced fragment from Monhegan's shore; *Sunday's* idler sits in the sun.

Gradually these anecdotal residues were subsumed and

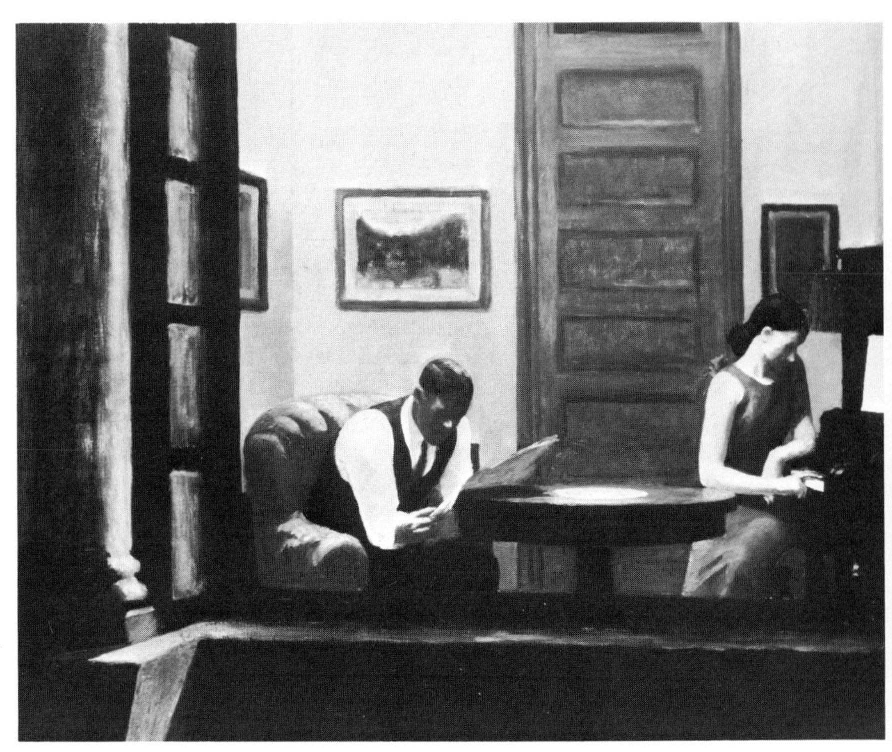

81 · Room in New York, 1932

put to service on behalf of the principal concern of Hopper's later years: light. He said that all he wanted to do was 'to paint sunlight on the side of a house'. He did far more than that, but light is at the heart of his project – light in relation to sentience.

His solitaries face the sun like people entranced. At first, in the early '30s, they were content merely to enjoy the light. Increasingly they seek it out and by the late '40s have become a race of sun-worshippers. A gilded statue caged behind bay windows in *August in the City* (1945) gazes upwards, directly into the face of the sun. A casual gardener in *Pennsylvania Coal Town* (1947) glances into a corridor of light between houses, his eye caught by some sudden revelation. *Summertime's* girl (1943) faces boldly into the wind and the sun. Others pay homage to the sky at morning, noon and evening – by filling stations, in hotel rooms, in lonely houses, in New York City, on Cape Cod, in Carolina, wherever the sun shines.

His figures are as though hypnotised by morning light, high noon and the last rays of evening. They have the look of communicants, absorbing the body of the light. An elderly man meditates by a partly-illumined window in *Hotel by a Railroad* (1952); his wife reads by a grey reflected light within the room. Detached from the entrancing sun Hopper's people turn to prosaic matters; they talk, read and muse to themselves, like the couple in *Room in New York* (1932), one engrossed in a newspaper and the other idly tapping on a piano; they confer and work late in the office, knowing that they will be bewitched by tomorrow's sun. The neon-lit night is a time for reflection, sociability and mere waiting – with, for instance, the casual clients in *Nighthawks* (1942).

This affair with the overwhelming sun is touched on by others: by the photographer Alfred Stieglitz who celebrates the white heights of New York; by the poet William Carlos Williams who, in *The Semblables,* redeems a dour suburban landscape and a society in thrall to hoary rituals with this exultant coda – 'But ranks/of brilliant car-tops row on row/give back in all his glory the/late November sun and hushed/attend, before that tumbled/ground . . .'

No one else, however, comes close to Hopper's intensity and thoroughness. He scrutinises the day and night, and notes especially those moments when darkness encroaches

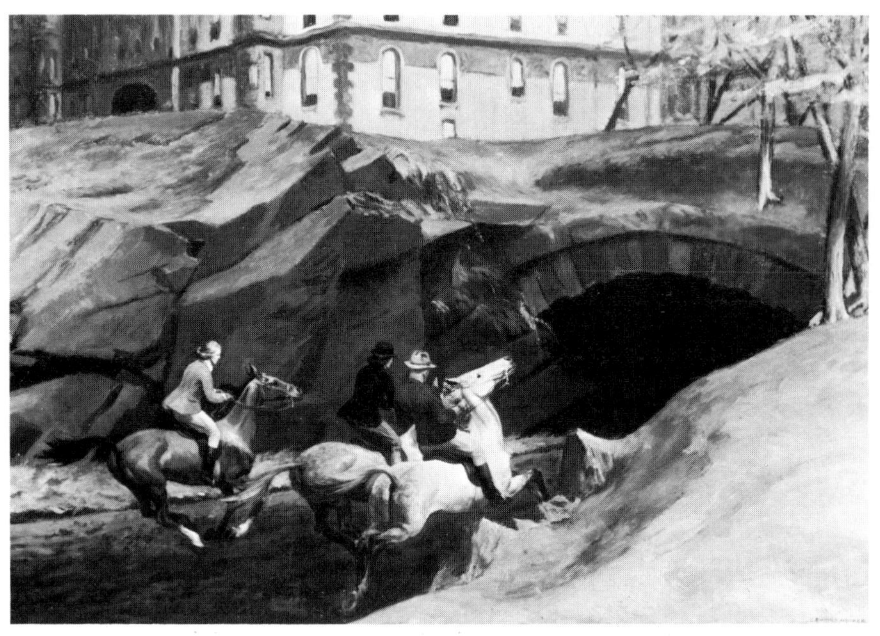

90 · Bridle Path, 1939

or lingers. His light is welcomed, and takes on meaning, against darkness which lurks in the trees in *Seven A.M.* (1948) and in *Cape Cod Morning* (1950). It is the morning light, intense on a white wall, which gives point to his *Dawn Before Gettysburg* (1934). The vivid gable serves as a foil to the huddled company down among the shadows and about to join Mathew Brady's casualties on the field of battle. In another Civil War painting an artillery column heads down a road into a tunnel of trees, into the same ominous darkness which scares the horses in *The Bridle Path* (1939) and greets a visitor at the mouth of another tunnel in *Approaching a City* (1946). Sunlight means life, full and untroubled – in unison with Nature. Elsewhere, under lamps and in shadows, lie routine chores, the small change of social life and ultimately the loss of a sense of oneself.

Hopper, a philosopher-painter, reflects on elemental matters, but he reflects obliquely, through others' experience. He paints like someone reluctant to claim first-hand experience. Others look into the light, never himself. In the '20s he found a figure for 'the boldness of ships' at a remove, in the set of a dormer window. In the '30s and after he honoured the sun through the obeisances paid by others. His American luminists are well on the way to being taken over by what they revere, and he resists that tendency in himself. He deals, he implies, only in pictures, in artificer's work which acknowledges Nature but keeps it at a distance. Once he comes close to looking into the heart of the light, in *Railroad, Sunset* (1929), but by then the sun has dipped out of the picture and the main figure against a ravishing sky is a signaller's box, a plain fabrication as well as a cautionary reminder of piecemeal normalcy. Moreover the sunset's drama is kept at a remove, on the other side of the tracks. Nature's splendours are approached with circumspection, in the '20s and after, by an artist who presents himself humbly as an artificer and reporter on others' visions.

According to reports he was a widely-read man. His wife depicted him, in 1955, reading a book by Robert Frost, and it is in Frost's poetry that he would have found confirmation for the oblique strategies he used in his own paintings. Frost wrote and observed from a distance, either retelling what others had told him or remembering and shaping his own experience to make a tale or moral of it. He too saw figures in doorways as he travelled by, and he too wondered over their larger meanings – like Hopper he wondered in a plain enough idiom to keep the ineffable at a decent distance, although it is this which preoccupies them both.

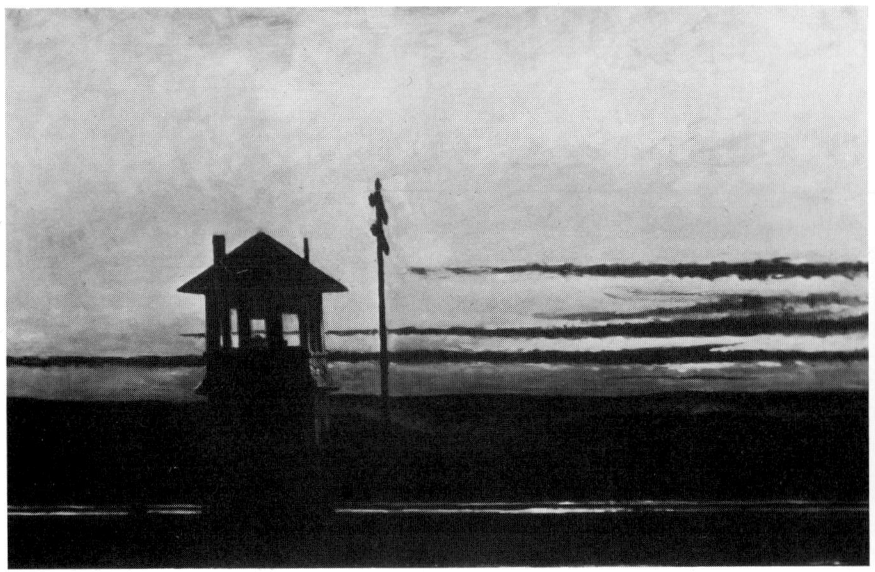

75 · Railroad, Sunset, 1929

The Figure in the Doorway

by Robert Frost

The grade surmounted, we were riding high
Through level mountains nothing to the eye
But scrub oak, scrub oak and the lack of earth
That kept the oaks from getting any girth.
But as through the monotony we ran,
We came to where there was a living man.
His great gaunt figure filled his cabin door,
And had he fallen inward on the floor,
He must have measured to the further wall.
But we who passed were not to see him fall.
The miles and miles he lived from anywhere
Were evidently something he could bear.
He stood unshaken, and if grim and gaunt,
It was not necessarily from want.
He had the oaks for heating and for light.
He had a hen, he had a pig in sight.
He had a well, he had the rain to catch.
He had a ten-by-twenty garden patch.
Nor did he lack for common entertainment.
That I assume was what our passing train meant.
He could look at us in our diner eating,
And if so moved uncurl a hand in greeting.

Reprinted from *The Poetry of Robert Frost,*
edited by Edward Connery Lathem, Jonathan Cape,
London 1971

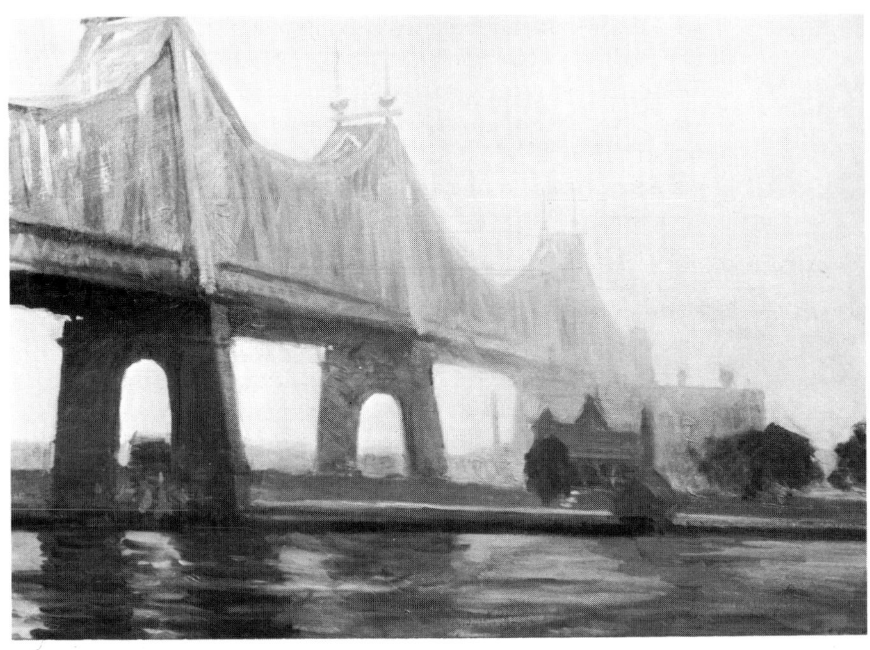

44 · Queensborough Bridge, 1913

Hopper's Vision of New York

by Alfred Kazin

In the days when Manhattan Bridge was still open to pedestrians, when you could stroll across the great Brooklyn Bridge without being taken hostage, when nothing in this world was such a gift as the light over the East River bursting into a BMT car and breaking up the boredom, I would regularly make my way between Manhattan and Brooklyn with the feeling that these halves of my life were joined not by ceaseless daily travel but by images drawn from paintings of New York.

I did not know I loved New York, I did not know there was a New York to love more than a neighbourhood, until I saw it in museums. The trouble with growing up in a Brooklyn tenement was not so much that you were poor – there was nothing but other people's poverty to compare yours with – but that the struggle for existence made everything else seem trivial, unworthy. The city fell on me every day like so much sleet, but I was unconscious of the subtler impressions it was making. Why was the dome of a certain savings bank – it bulked on the horizon like a cathedral as the subway moved into the open across Manhattan Bridge – so dramatic? Why, long before I saw the photographs of Alfred Stieglitz and Joseph Stella's overdesigned paintings, did the crisscrossing supports of Brooklyn Bridge haunt me? Why did the rows of brownstones just south of Washington Square and west of Fifth Avenue seem to me more comforting and healing than any image of green fields?

I had no genial New York images of my own until I discovered John Sloan in the old American Wing of the Metropolitan Museum of Art, Reginald Marsh in the Whitney Museum of American Art when it was on Eighth Street, forgotten prints of Columbia Heights in the Brooklyn Museum. New York's painters seemed to love the city more than its writers did; they were as romantically

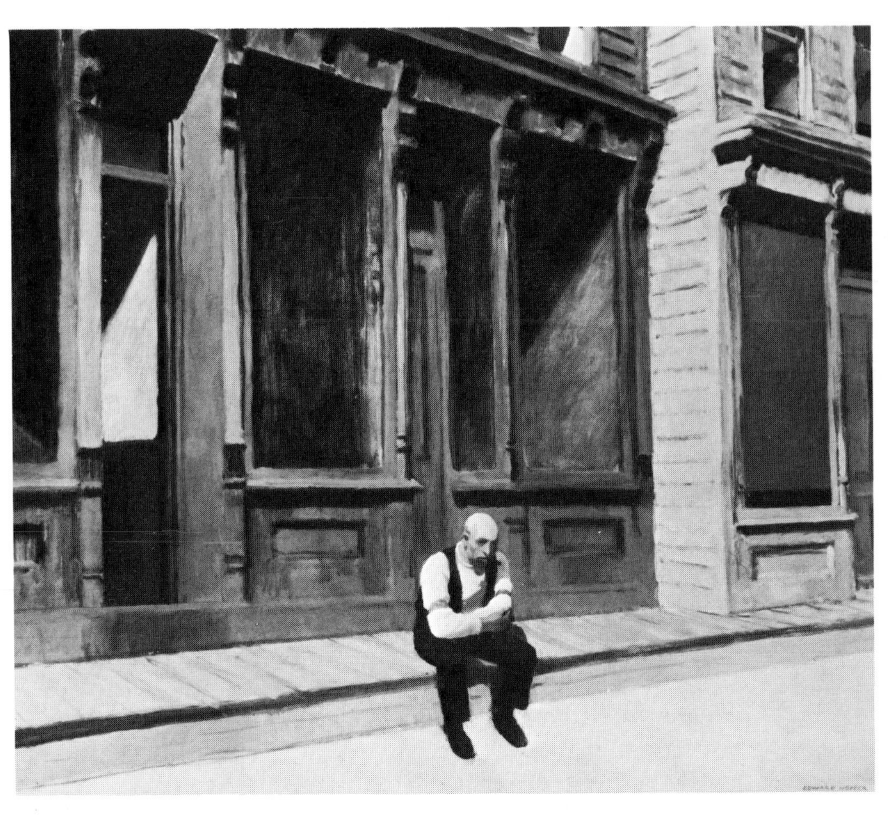

69 · Sunday, 1926

tuned in to the passing show as fashion photographers. Fondly coloured impressions of the crowds at rush hour under the old El. Brownstones and the old, low, red-brick storefronts. Decorative stone and wire and glass whose weight in the city had always hit me like a blow. The rooftops where the toughies in my neighbourhood trained racing pigeons and undernourished Jewish featherweights sparred on the gravel before they got knocked out of the ring at Canarsie. The roof edges across which I had actually seen cops chase robbers. The air shafts and chimney pots that were so 'pictorial' in paintings sweetly overlooked, in my daily life, what I knew as the subway huddle, the heat, the reports by terrified storekeepers of threats by Lepke Buchalter and Gurrah Shapiro of Murder Inc. No painter depicted what I knew as the unheard scream in the crowd when city marshals threw furniture out on the street during an eviction.

New York painters brought my chaotic secret impressions into the light. An unconscious watcher came to life one day and began to describe the city of his endless prowling. But, of course, these middle-class painters bravely facing the commonplace and the ugly were as sentimental about the city as earlier painters had been about the Hudson River Valley. They thought Klein's, the grimy, cheap-dress emporium in Union Square, was so picture-worthy that it was almost beautiful. My favourite memory of Klein's was a crude drawing just inside the store of a weeping girl behind bars: 'Don't Bring Disgrace To Your Family By Shoplifting?' I was amused by Reginald Marsh's bouncy ballets of shoppers along 14th Street. Someone had actually painted 14th Street instead of just surviving it – as my father barely survived when, at his local of the International Brotherhood of Painters, Decorators and Paperhangers, he voted, for once in his life, against the union despot, a charmer known even to his family as 'Jake the Bum.'

None of the people in these New York paintings ever seemed to me more than symbols, shakily sketched in with other symbols to afford recognition. You know – the New York crowd! There was a certain hastiness to urban American painting that no doubt reflected the excited discovery of New York as a subject. Like so many American realistic novelists – Frank Norris, for example – most New York painters were more at home with sweating muscles than with the puzzle of existence. But I was grateful for the painters of the 'Ashcan' school – they gave dignity to a New York I knew as harsh, merciless, exhausting. Time after time I would stand amazed by what a picture would bring home to me. Someone had seen a design in New York's bridges and rooftops that locked my whirling city into a frame. A charm essentially wistful softened even the stabbing outlines of New York skyscrapers and made familiarity an aesthetic fact. What the 'Ashcan' fellows saw, now I could remember having seen.

There was one exception to these cosy, picturesque painters of New York: Edward Hopper. Unlike so many American paintings just before and after World War II, 'representational' and 'abstract' alike, his work was not slapdash, hurried, theatrically self-conscious. The immensely tall, immensely quiet man I often saw walking in Greenwich Village and in the moors of South Truro on Cape Cod seemed tensely alone; he reminded me of Virginia Woolf's impression of Robinson Crusoe – 'a man staring at a pot.'

Hopper for me was like his unprecedented paintings of solitary people staring at the glass in New York bedrooms, coffee shops and offices. Perhaps he had taken the advice of the philosopher Wittgenstein: 'Don't think! LOOK!' Yet you could not have guessed what the handsome man was looking at as he edged his way through Washington Square Park. His figures never looked *through* the glass they were facing. Their masked, identical, hawklike faces were concentrated in thought unavailable to anyone, perhaps especially to themselves.

Hopper and his work lacked the audience-grabbing extremism that disconcerts me when I enter many exhibitions of late 20th-century American painting. 'Hey, everybody! Look what I'm into *this* week!' The solidity of objects in Hopper's paintings contrasts with the evanescence of so much in urban *and* rural America; only Hopper could have lived and worked in the same walk-up on Washington Square for 54 years. Yet he was hardly under the illusion that what he liked would stay around. What saved him from the jitters of incessant replacement – of people even more than of one's favourite buildings – was his not being topical. He was not a 'social' painter or thinker; he was happily free of 'ideas.' What absorbed him in the course of a long life and arduous career were certain repetitious themes: a single figure in a bare room, restaurant, theatre; bridges and roofs without a person in the picture to recall the unseen watcher brooding over the thickness and hardness of building materials. It all was beautifully 'personal.' As this most unwilling talker among American painters admitted on the occasion of his 1933 retrospective at the Museum of Modern Art, 'My aim in painting has always been the most exact transcription possible of my most intimate impressions of nature.'

This sounds like Emerson or Robert Frost, two of Hopper's favourite writers. In the light of what Hopper actually accomplished in still-reverberating paintings that show no essential difference in style or interest from 1924, when his work finally began to sell, to his death at the age of 85 in 1967, it has to be said that, for once, a painter's 'big' statement described exactly what he sought – and achieved – in the realm of his own mind.

Gail Levin, the associate curator of the Whitney's Hopper collection, says in her new book, 'Edward Hopper: The Art and the Artist,' that Hopper carried in his wallet this quotation from Goethe: 'The beginning and end of all literary activity is the reproduction of the world that surrounds me by means of the world that is in me, all things being grasped, related, recreated, moulded and reconstructed in a personal form and an original manner.' This is the kind of high-flying claim for one's own sacred 'Me' that is Emerson's bequest to American writers and painters. From Thoreau, who lived it, to Clyfford Still, who just talked about it, Americans have never been able to resist the transcendentalist religion. But Hopper, as the haunting expressiveness of places in his work reveals (the people in his paintings are something else), achieved a personal transaction with the exterior American world that everyone who looks at 'Early Sunday Morning' or 'House by the Railroad' or 'Chop Suey' can take into himself as an equally personal experience.

What happens in these paintings, what is still happening when I look at them, is that Hopper's mind has incorporated something 'outside' into itself. And in such a way as to make unforgettable this sense we have of being occupied by nothing but our own consciousness. We are

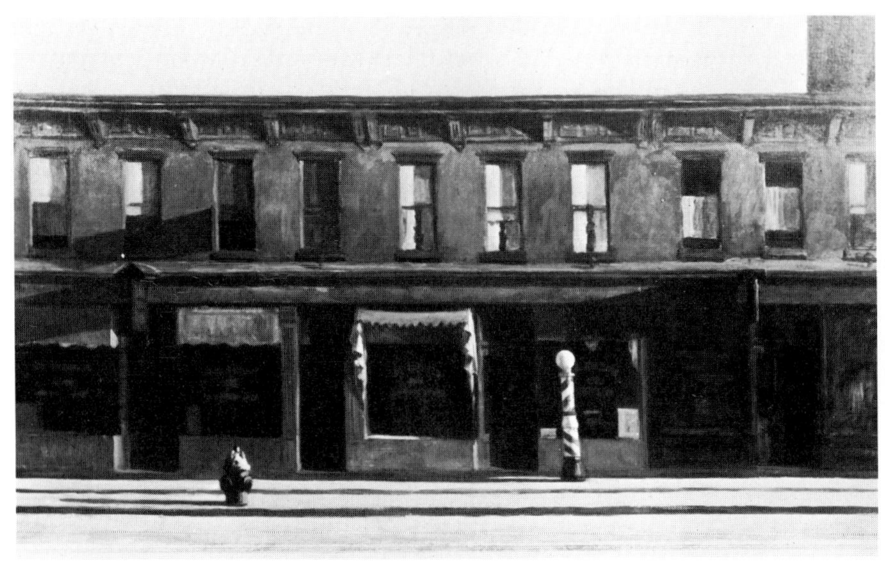

77 · Early Sunday Morning, 1930

dominated and concentrated by a particular image in all the solidity and exactness available to our senses. Everything happens within and because of our single consciousness. What makes such paintings 'unique,' 'memorable' and 'haunting' is that the bond between Hopper and certain buildings has become restrictive of everything else. Why, in 'Early Sunday Morning' (Hopper did not call it that – he originally titled it 'Seventh Avenue Shops' – but you can see why the absolute silence of the street would lead other people to think of Sunday in certain parts of New York), do the hydrant, the barber pole and the row of low, red-brick houses that Hopper saw on lower Seventh Avenue have such depth? Why does the *bulk* of these humanless houses rivet us, finally telling us what the unseen watcher has so long and unconsciously seen in them? Why does that complicated Victorian house 'by the railroad' so fascinate us? It is not because the house is 'typically American'; Thomas Hart Benton, John Steuart Curry, even the more interesting Charles Burchfield, whom Hopper generously admired, never painted anything with this thoroughness. The fascination of the best of Hopper's paintings is that, in each of them, something outside of him has come to seem the style of his own perception. Just as philosophers discovered the nature of thinking by realizing that we do not really 'see' anything that does not resemble the innate forms in which we think, so achievement in any art lies in the ability to recreate the 'world' into something that the mind feels totally at home with, that it ultimately welcomes as a further aspect of itself.

The shining new American Wing at the Metropolitan Museum contains Hopper's 'Office in a Small City.' There is the usually decorous, taut American figure in an office; the face gives away nothing of what it may have absorbed from its surroundings. I suspect the man has absorbed nothing. Hopper was an indifferent psychologist, far more interested in architecture than in the human drama contained in offices as well as bedrooms. (Even his bedrooms often show only one figure.) The man in 'Office in a Small City,' like so many of Hopper's duplicate figures, is there to stiffen the already tight concentration with which a section of the external building frames the office box and the man at his desk. The most remarkable detail

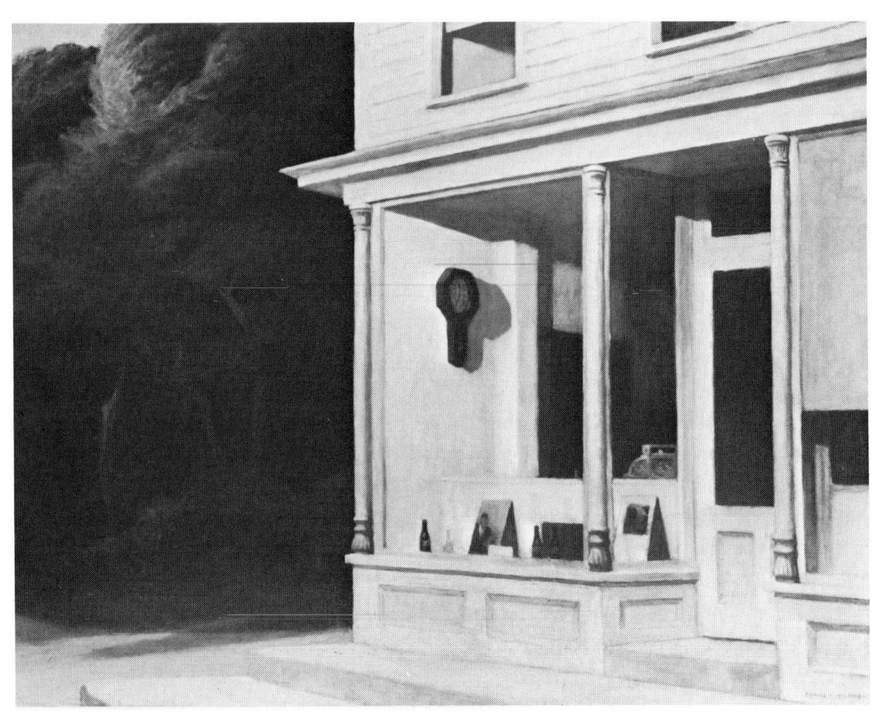

102 · Seven A.M., 1948

in this picture is the great white rectangle into which the outside of the building has been solidified, illuminated, purified. It bestrides the office with marvellous force.

The caption for this painting informs us that Hopper achieved 'purely objective presentations of people and places, with no traces discernible of the way they made him feel. His observations are as impersonal as those of a camera's lens. . . .' Of course, no one, least of all the photographer peering through a camera, achieves 'purely objective presentations.' Even painters who tried for the impersonality of a diagram or blueprint, like the precisionist Charles Sheeler, were as personal as the rest of us. What is distressing in this caption is the typical American confusion between the personal in feeling and the personal in thought. Very few painters or writers or, for that matter, scientists get down to the irreducible and untranslatable experience of their own independent thought – of being able to keep what they alone have thought. Emerson said that in the works of others we recognize, too late, our own rejected thoughts. The only meaning of 'originality' can be a mind that, like Hopper's, is unable to dodge the overwhelmingness of the great white rectangle of light in 'Office in a Small City.' In 'Early Sunday Morning,' Hopper could not rest with the amazement of total silence on lower Seventh Avenue. He had to put that silence into the hydrant, the barber pole, that dark red row of houses.

For years after World War II, walking every day past a certain stretch of dark red houses on Fulton Street in Brooklyn Heights, I was convinced that here and nowhere else was the street wrapped in early-morning shadows that Hopper had seen. Even when I learned that Hopper had found his subject in Manhattan, I claimed his wonderfully strong, concentrated mass of New York City silence for Brooklyn and myself. The painting convinced me that telepathy can occur between a picture and its viewer. The passage from Hopper's street to my mind moved me more than any other image of New York. It was the silence that got me, for it is just such silence that a writer or painter, that unseen watcher, can live in for years, not even knowing all that he is thinking about when he is alone with a street.

Edward Hopper was the real thing, the artist who

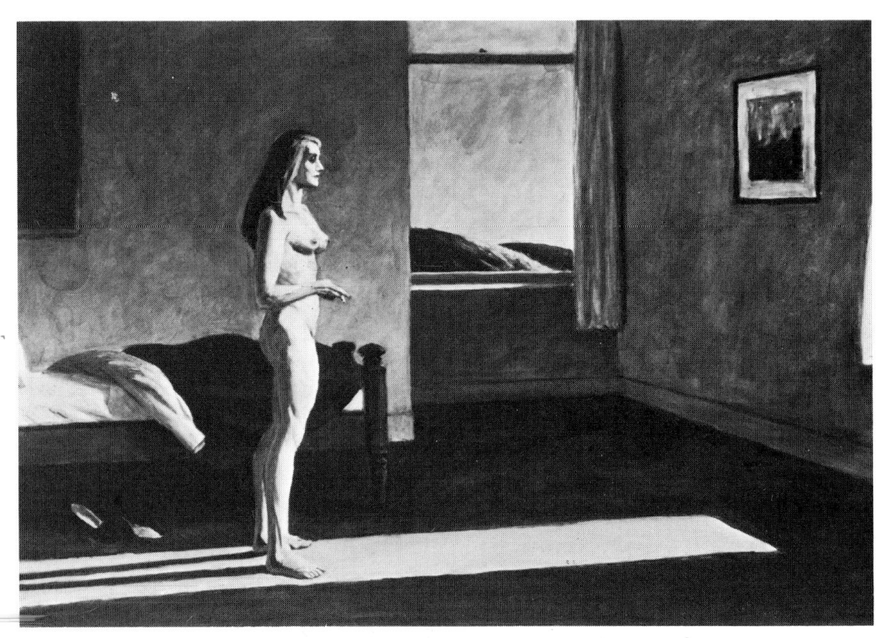

111 · A Woman in the Sun, 1961

becomes nothing but his vision of things. His art has a distinctness and depth that remind me of F. Scott Fitzgerald's remark about his own work: it had 'the stamp that goes into my books so you can read it blind like Braille.' Hopper lived a conscientious life. I saw him frequently without ever thinking to talk to him. It seemed absurd to confront that utterly reserved figure sitting with his wife, Jo, over hamburgers in Riker's on Seventh Avenue near Barrow Street.

Hopper was never easy with himself or the American world that he made a piece of himself. He was in his early 40's before his work began to sell and he was able to give up illustrating advertisements and magazine fiction and to marry. He hated illustrating when 'what I wanted to do was to paint sunlight on the side of a house.' Eventually, he became famous, a particular favourite of the Whitney Museum, where Lloyd Goodrich, director of the museum from 1958-68, did so much to present and explain Hopper until the art world was ready for him. Hopper was shown at the Whitney Studio Club even before there was a Whitney Museum on Eighth Street. He was later honoured by a long series of one-man shows and retrospectives. But to the end of his life at 3 Washington Square North, where he doggedly carried up coal to heat the pot-bellied stove in his studio, he remained the laborious, taciturn, frugal fellow from Nyack, N.Y., whose father was in dry goods.

Jo Nivison Hopper died in 1968, a year after her husband. she had kept a careful record of his work and had played a major role in it, for she insisted on posing for every female figure in his paintings. Theirs was a long, close, difficult marriage; Jo was a fellow artist less talented and successful than her husband. She hated to cook, which is why one so often saw the Hoppers in Village coffee shops and cheap restaurants. The vaguely melancholy man preferred not to talk at all unless he absolutely had to; the little woman with the ponytail never stopped.

What first startled me more than anything else in Hopper's paintings was the absence of the superficially drawn crowd that New York's romantic realists went in for. Even when a man and woman are shown together (and this was Hopper's idea of a crowd), there is some unexplained tension between them. His couples are

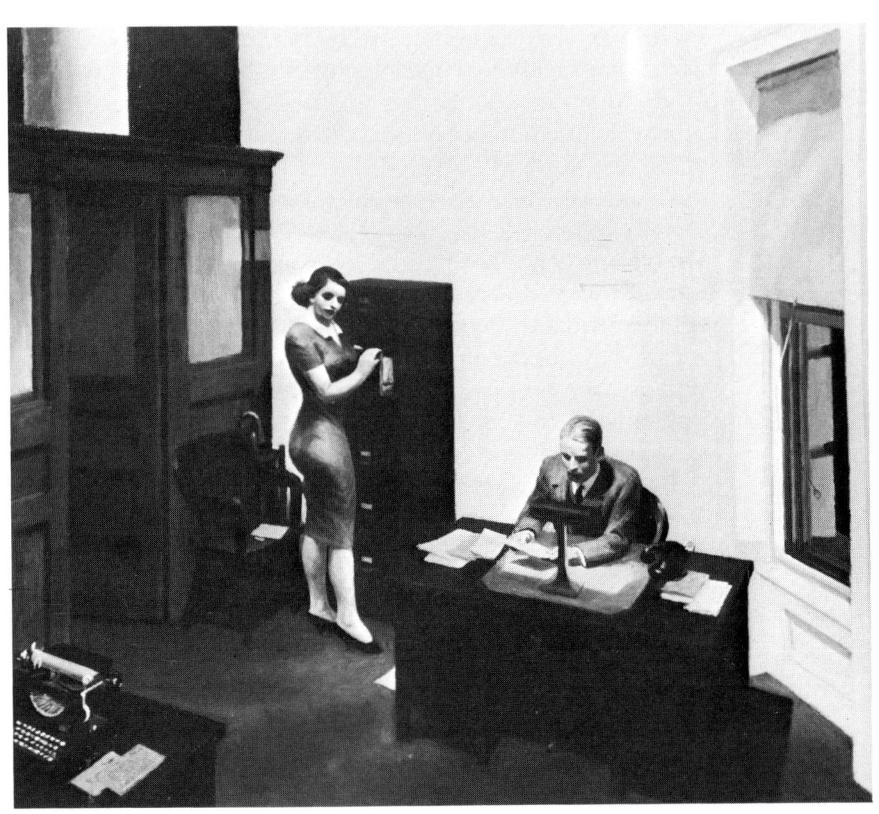

95 · Office at Night, 1940

joined only by a mysterious silence, together only in the sense that they are stiffly alike. 'Excursion Into Philosophy,' for instance shows a man, dressed and sitting disconsolately with a book on the edge of a bed, while behind him the figure of a woman, outstretched with her back to him, indicates some disappointment or rejection.

But most often in Hopper's paintings there is that famous single figure – often a female, nude or partially undressed – that has imposed on his work so many associations with 'loneliness.' Apparently, to be alone for a minute in this country is to seem 'lonely' – at least to others. Hopper complained that, in discussions of his work, the 'loneliness thing was overdone.' What obviously obsessed him was not 'loneliness' but the taut surface of some deeply engrained solitude. Even the solitary women rejoicing in the Cape Cod sunshine are as facially inexpressive – or taciturn – as the supposedly troubled woman in 'Eleven A.M.' Hopper's self-portraits are so warm and even buoyant that I suspect, in painting women, he diluted his sympathy with old-fashioned decorum. *Everyone* in a Hopper painting shows decorum, even when alone.

Hopper's pictures have often been compared to stages: Something is about to happen. But he was no dramatist. What he generally gives us is a repetition of bleak psychic exchange. I know that in 'Office at Night' the secretary standing in front of the file cabinet and her employer woodenly seated at his desk (she is looking straight at him but he is immersed in his papers) are supposed to be emotionally involved. But the involvement, if it exists because they are together after hours, does not get beyond some elementary tension. Like so many 'dramas' in Hopper, this one is silent and mysteriously grumpy. The rooms and the buildings and the roofs talk more than the people do, and talk *for* them.

This lack of extensive human drama is not a failure, but it is a limitation. Hopper is a truly good painter, but no more than any other American painter is he a great one, on a par with, say, Matisse. His emotional world is too anxiously at a standstill. How often do we see his people looking at a window that is more interesting than they are? And through the window, beyond the building, the light is magnificent. Oh, that Hopper light! He caught the peculiar need for it in the crowded city, and he caught the relief of its abundance when he got out of the city to the New England coast.

Looking at the happy shock of all that light on the water in his paintings of Cape Cod, we find ourselves thirsting for light as if it were water. Hopper is in an old American line – he is the poet-painter of our total physical environment, the immediate skin of habitations and weather next to our own skin. The people moving about in those buildings and in that weather are really part of them. They have no life apart from these 'forces'; they are wholly submissive to their material lives. And such submissiveness is too often the theme of our lives.

This article first appeared in *The New York Times Magazine* on 7 September, 1980 and is reprinted here by kind permission of the author and the publishers.

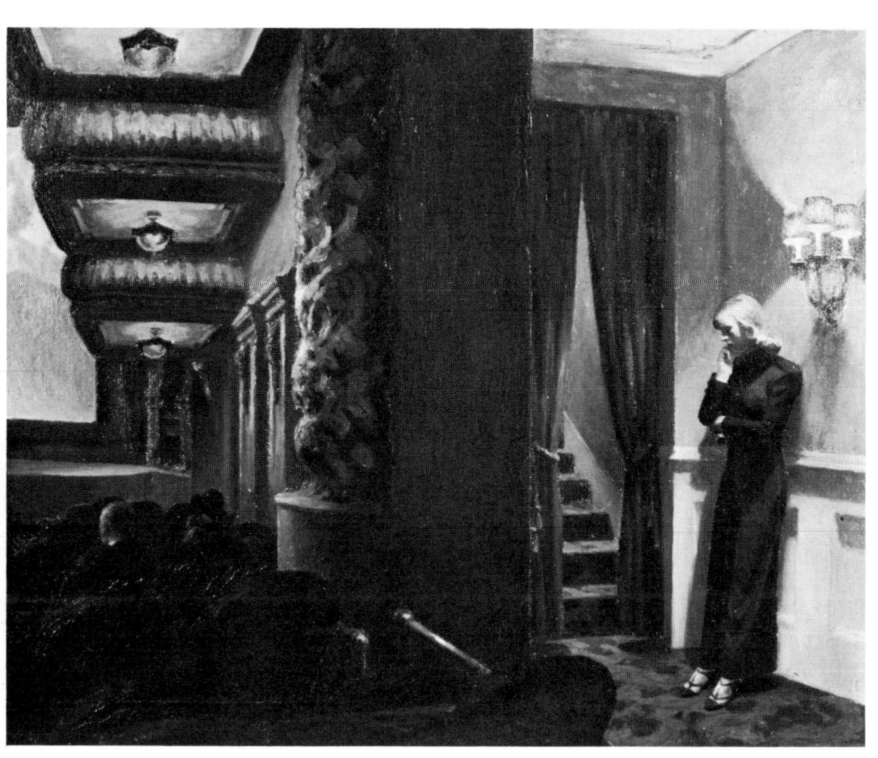

89 · New York Movie, 1939

Great art is the outward expression of an inner life in the artist, and this inner life will result in his personal vision of the world. No amount of skillful invention can replace the essential element of imagination. One of the weaknesses of much abstract painting is the attempt to substitute the inventions of the intellect for a pristine imaginative conception.

The inner life of a human being is a vast and varied realm and does not concern itself alone with stimulating arrangements of color, form and design.

The term 'life' as used in art is something not to be held in contempt, for it implies all of existence, and the province of art is to react to it and not to shun it.

Painting will have to deal more fully and less obliquely with life and nature's phenomena before it can again become great.

Edward Hopper,
from 'Statements by Four Artists',
Reality, 1, New York, 1953.

Catalogue

Plate references are given for the monograph *Edward Hopper: The Art and The Artist* by Gail Levin (see Bibliography). Paintings marked with an asterisk are reproduced in this publication.
All measurements are given in inches.

PAINTINGS

1
[Painter and Model], c.1902-4
oil on board
10¼ × 8¹⁄₁₆
Whitney Museum of American Art, New York; Bequest of Josephine N. Hopper 70.1420
(plate 73)

2
[Solitary Figure in a Theatre], c.1902-4
oil on board
12½ × 9⁹⁄₁₆
Whitney Museum of American Art, New York; Bequest of Josephine N. Hopper 70.1418
(plate 335)

3
[Standing Nude], c.1902-6
oil on canvas
22⅛ × 15
Whitney Museum of American Art, New York; Bequest of Josephine N. Hopper 70.1269

4
[Self-Portrait], 1903
oil on canvas
14 × 10
Whitney Museum of American Art, New York; Bequest of Josephine N. Hopper 70.1650
(plate 11)

5
[Artist's Bedroom, Nyack], c.1903-6
oil on board
15¹⁄₁₆ × 11¹⁄₁₆
Whitney Museum of American Art, New York; Bequest of Josephine N. Hopper 70.1412
(plate 30)

6
[Self-Portrait], c.1904-5
oil on board
16¹⁵⁄₁₆ × 12¹⁵⁄₁₆
Whitney Museum of American Art, New York; Bequest of Josephine N. Hopper 70.1410
(plate 14)

7
[Self-Portrait], c.1904-6
oil on canvas
20 × 16
Thyssen-Bornemisza Collection, Lugano-Castagnola, Switzerland
(plate 15)

8
[Self-Portrait], c.1904-6
oil on canvas
26 × 22
Whitney Museum of American Art, New York; Bequest of Josephine N. Hopper 70.1253
(plate 12)

9
[Self-Portrait], c.1904-6
oil on canvas
28 × 17¹⁵⁄₁₆
Whitney Museum of American Art, New York; Bequest of Josephine N. Hopper 70.1254
(plate 13)

10
[Bridge in Paris], 1906
oil on wood
9⅝ × 13
Whitney Museum of American Art, New York; Bequest of Josephine N. Hopper 70.1305
(plate 84)

11
[Group of Men in an Orchestra Pit], before 1906
oil on canvas
15 × 20
Whitney Museum of American Art, New York; Bequest of Josephine N. Hopper 70.1243

12
[Interior Courtyard at 48 rue de Lille, Paris], 1906
oil on wood
13 × 9⅝
Whitney Museum of American Art, New York; Bequest of Josephine N. Hopper 70.1304
(plate 83)

13
[Paris Street], 1906
oil on wood
13 × 10
Whitney Museum of American Art, New York; Bequest of Josephine N. Hopper 70.1296
(plate 81)

14
[Stairway at 48 rue de Lille, Paris], 1906
oil on wood
13 × 9¼
Whitney Museum of American Art, New York; Bequest of Josephine N. Hopper 70.1295
(plate 82)

15
[Still Life with Earthenware Jug], before 1906
oil on canvas
22$\frac{3}{16}$ × 18$\frac{1}{16}$
Whitney Museum of American Art, New York; Bequest of Josephine N. Hopper 70.1261

16
Le Pont des Arts, 1907
oil on canvas
23$\frac{1}{16}$ × 28$\frac{1}{16}$
Whitney Museum of American Art, New York; Bequest of Josephine N. Hopper 70.1181
(plate 103)

17
Pont du Carrousel in the Fog, 1907
oil on canvas
23¼ × 28¼
Whitney Museum of American Art, New York; Bequest of Josephine N. Hopper 70.1245
(plate 100)

18
Après-midi de juin or L'après-midi de printemps, 1907
oil on canvas
23½ × 28½
Whitney Museum of American Art, New York; Bequest of Josephine N. Hopper 70.1172
(plate 102)

19
Gateway and Fence, St Cloud, 1907
oil on canvas
23 × 28
Whitney Museum of American Art, New York; Bequest of Josephine N. Hopper 70.1231
(plate 105)

20
Les Lavoirs à Pont Royal, 1907
oil on canvas
23¼ × 28½
Whitney Museum of American Art, New York; Bequest of Josephine N. Hopper 70.1247
(plate 107)

21
Le Louvre et la Seine, 1907
oil on canvas
23½ × 28½
Whitney Museum of American Art, New York; Bequest of Josephine N. Hopper 70.1186
(plate 101)

22
Notre Dame de Paris, 1907
oil on canvas
23½ × 28½
Whitney Museum of American Art, New York; Bequest of Josephine N. Hopper 70.1179
(plate 108)

23
Le Parc de St Cloud, 1907
oil on canvas
23½ × 28½
Whitney Museum of American Art, New York; Bequest of Josephine N. Hopper 70.1180
(plate 106)

24
Trees in Sunlight, Parc de St Cloud, 1907
oil on canvas
23⅝ × 28¾
Whitney Museum of American Art, New York; Bequest of Josephine N. Hopper 70.1248
(plate 423)

25
The El Station, 1908
oil on canvas
20 × 29
Whitney Museum of American Art, New York; Bequest of Josephine N. Hopper 70.1182
(plate 261)

26
Tug Boat with Black Smokestack, c.1908
oil on canvas
20 × 29
Whitney Museum of American Art, New York; Bequest of Josephine N. Hopper 70.1192
(plate 121)

27
Valley of the Seine, 1908
oil on canvas
26 × 38
Whitney Museum of American Art, New York; Bequest of Josephine N. Hopper 70.1183
(plate 120)

28
Le Quai des Grands Augustins, 1909
oil on canvas
23½ × 28½
Whitney Museum of American Art, New York; Bequest of Josephine N. Hopper 70.1173
(plate 119)

29
Riverboat, 1909
oil on canvas
28 × 48
Whitney Museum of American Art, New York; Bequest of Josephine N. Hopper 70.1190
(plate 113)

30
Le Bistro or **The Wine Shop,** 1909
oil on canvas
23⅜ × 28½
Whitney Museum of American Art, New York; Bequest of Josephine N. Hopper 70.1187
(plate 122)

31
Ile Saint-Louis or **La Cité,** 1909
oil on canvas
23¾ × 28½
Whitney Museum of American Art, New York; Bequest of Josephine N. Hopper 70.1177
(plate 112)

32
The Louvre in a Thunder Storm, 1909
oil on canvas
23 × 28¾
Whitney Museum of American Art, New York; Bequest of Josephine N. Hopper 70.1223
(plate 116)

33
Le Pavillon de Flore, 1909
oil on canvas
23½ × 28½
Whitney Museum of American Art, New York; Bequest of Josephine N. Hopper 70.1174
(plate 115)

34
Le Pont Neuf or **Ecluse de la Monnaie,** 1909
oil on canvas
23¼ × 28
Whitney Museum of American Art, New York; Bequest of Josephine N. Hopper 70.1178
(plate 118)

35
Summer Interior, 1909
oil on canvas
24 × 29
Whitney Museum of American Art, New York; Bequest of Josephine N. Hopper 70.1197
(plate 123)

36
Blackwell's Island, 1911
oil on canvas
24 × 29
Whitney Museum of American Art, New York; Bequest of Josephine N. Hopper 70.1188
(plate 124)

37
Squam Light, 1912
oil on canvas
24 × 29
Private Collection
(plate 128)

38
American Village, 1912
oil on canvas
26 × 38
Whitney Museum of American Art, New York; Bequest of Josephine N. Hopper 70.1185
(plate 130)

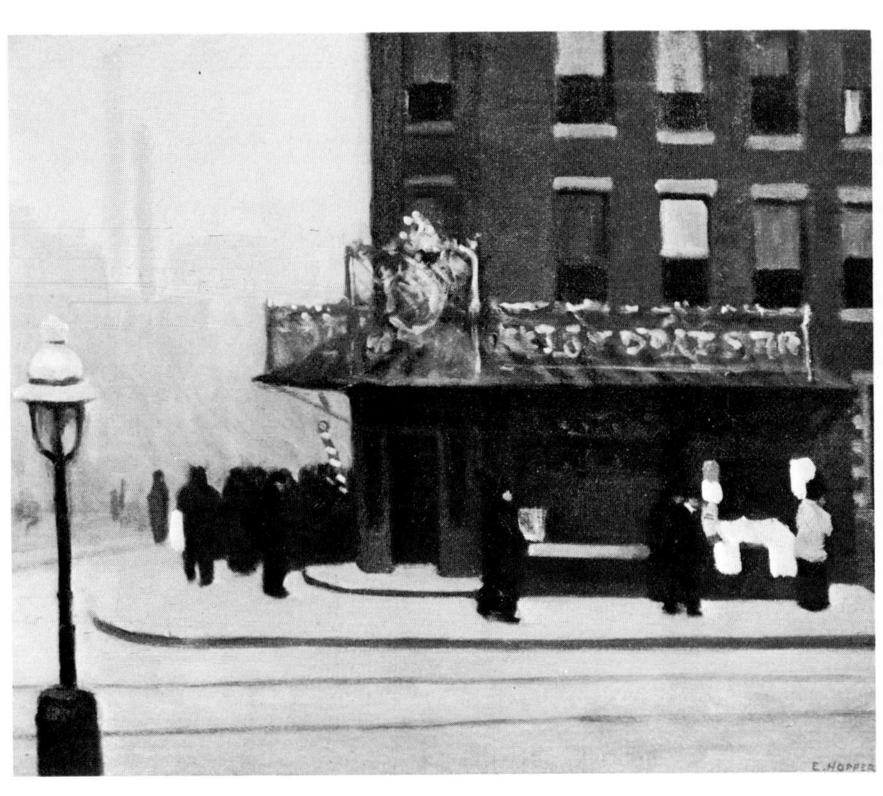

43 · New York Corner or Corner Saloon, 1913

39
Briar Neck, 1912
oil on canvas
24 × 29
Whitney Museum of American Art, New York;
Bequest of Josephine N. Hopper 70.1193
(plate 129)

40
Gloucester Harbour, 1912
oil on canvas
26 × 38
Whitney Museum of American Art, New York;
Bequest of Josephine N. Hopper 70.1204
(plate 126)

41*
Italian Quarter, Gloucester, 1912
oil on canvas
23⅜ × 28½
Whitney Museum of American Art, New York;
Bequest of Josephine N. Hopper 70.1214
(plate 196)

42
Tall Masts, Gloucester, 1912
oil on canvas
24 × 29
Whitney Museum of American Art, New York;
Bequest of Josephine N. Hopper 70.1198
(plate 127)

43*
New York Corner or Corner Saloon, 1913
oil on canvas
24 × 29
The Museum of Modern Art, New York;
Abby Aldrich Rockefeller Fund, 1941
(plate 233)

44*
Queensborough Bridge, 1913
oil on canvas
25½ × 37½
Whitney Museum of American Art, New York;
Bequest of Josephine N. Hopper 70.1184
(plate 232)

45
Road in Maine, 1914
oil on canvas
24 × 29
Whitney Museum of American Art, New York;
Bequest of Josephine N. Hopper 70.1201
(plate 131)

46
Rocks and Houses, Ogunquit, 1914
oil on canvas
23¾ × 28¾
Whitney Museum of American Art, New York;
Bequest of Josephine N. Hopper 70.1202
(plate 132)

47
The Dories, Ogunquit, 1914
oil on canvas
24 × 29
Whitney Museum of American Art, New York;
Bequest of Josephine N. Hopper 70.1196
(plate 133)

48
[**Sea at Ogunquit**], 1914
oil on canvas
24¼ × 29⅛
Whitney Museum of American Art, New York;
Bequest of Josephine N. Hopper 70.1195
(plate 135)

49*
Soir Bleu, 1914
oil on canvas
36 × 72
Whitney Museum of American Art, New York;
Bequest of Josephine N. Hopper 70.1208
(plate 378)

50
[**Lighthouse**], c.1916
oil on board
9½ × 12¾
Private Collection
(plate 189)

51
Yonkers or **Summer Street,** 1916
oil on canvas
24 × 29
Whitney Museum of American Art, New York;
Bequest of Josephine N. Hopper 70.1215
(plate 234)

52
[**Bluff**], 1916-19
oil on board
9½ × 12
Whitney Museum of American Art, New York;
Bequest of Josephine N. Hopper 70.1319
(plate 147)

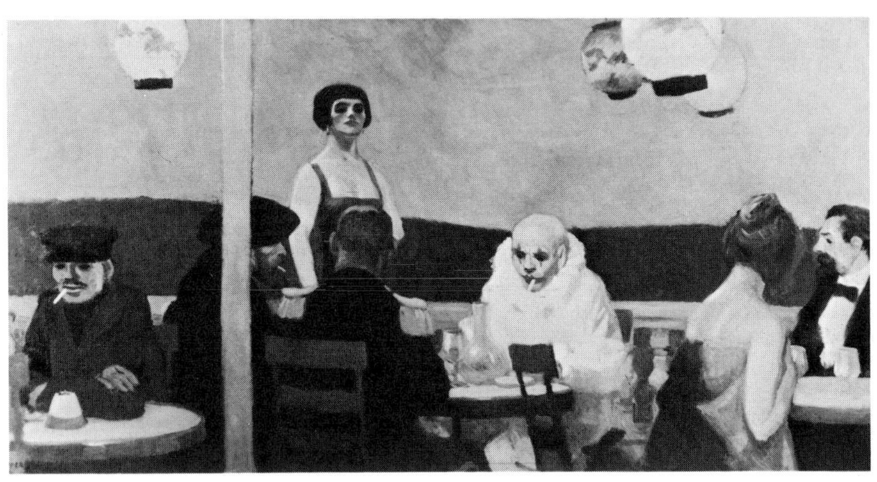

49 · Soir Bleu, 1914

53
Blackhead, Monhegan, 1916-19
oil on wood
9⅜ × 13
Whitney Museum of American Art, New York; Bequest of Josephine N. Hopper 70.1668
(plate 143)

54
Blackhead, Monhegan, 1916-19
oil on wood
9½ × 13
Whitney Museum of American Art, New York; Bequest of Josephine N. Hopper 70.1317
(plate 140)

55
Little Cove, Monhegan, 1916-19
oil on board
9 7/16 × 13
Whitney Museum of American Art, New York; Bequest of Josephine N. Hopper 70.1669
(plate 144)

56
[Rocky Cliffs by the Sea], 1916-19
oil on canvas
9⅜ × 12¾
Whitney Museum of American Art, New York; Bequest of Josephine N. Hopper 70.1675
(plate 153)

57
[Rocky Projection at the Sea], 1916-19
oil on board
9 × 12⅞
Whitney Museum of American Art, New York; Bequest of Josephine N. Hopper 70.1310
(plate 152)

58
[Rocky Seashore], 1916-19
oil on canvas
9½ × 12 15/16
Whitney Museum of American Art, New York; Bequest of Josephine N. Hopper 70.1666
(plate 150)

59
[Rocky Shore], 1916-19
oil on wood
9½ × 13
Whitney Museum of American Art, New York; Bequest of Josephine N. Hopper 70.1309
(plate 146)

60
[Rocky Shoreline], 1916-19
oil on board
9½ × 12⅞
Whitney Museum of American Art, New York; Bequest of Josephine N. Hopper 70.1672
(plate 145)

61
[Landscape with Fence and Trees], 1916-19
oil on canvas
9 7/16 × 12¾
Whitney Museum of American Art, New York; Bequest of Josephine N. Hopper 70.1667
(plate 138)

62
[Elizabeth Griffiths Smith Hopper, The Artist's Mother], 1916-20
oil on canvas
38 × 32
Whitney Museum of American Art, New York; Bequest of Josephine N. Hopper 70.1191
(plate 25)

63
Park Entrance, c.1918-20
oil on canvas
24 × 29
Whitney Museum of American Art, New York; Bequest of Josephine N. Hopper 70.1194
(plate 235)

64
[Girl at Sewing Machine], c.1921
oil on canvas
19 × 18
Thyssen-Bornemisza Collection, Lugano-Castagnola, Switzerland.
(plate 158)

65
New York Pavements, 1924
oil on canvas
24 × 29
The Chrysler Museum, Norfolk, Virginia; On loan from the collection of Walter P. Chrysler, Jr.
(*not exhibited*)

66
Apartment Houses, 1924
oil on canvas
25½ × 31½
Courtesy of The Pennsylvania Academy of the Fine Arts, Philadelphia; Lambert Fund Purchase, 1925
(plate 157)

67
[Stairway], c.1925
oil on wood
16 × 11⅞
Whitney Museum of American Art, New York;
Bequest of Josephine N. Hopper 70.1265
(plate 212)

68 *
[Self-Portrait], 1925-30
oil on canvas
25$\frac{1}{16}$ × 20⅜
Whitney Museum of American Art, New York;
Bequest of Josephine N. Hopper 70.1165
(plate 20)

69 *
Sunday, 1926
oil on canvas
29 × 34
The Phillips Collection, Washington, DC
(plate 160)

70 *
Lighthouse Hill, 1927
oil on canvas
28¼ × 39½
Dallas Museum of Fine Arts;
Gift of Mr and Mrs Maurice Purnell
(plate 193)

71
Hodgkin's House, Cape Ann, Massachusetts, 1928
oil on canvas
28 × 36
Private Collection;
Courtesy of Andrew Crispo Gallery, New York
(plate 218)

72
Chop Suey, 1929
oil on canvas
32⅛ × 38⅛
Collection of Barney A. Ebsworth
(plate 328)

73
The Lighthouse at Two Lights, 1929
oil on canvas
29½ × 43¼
The Metropolitan Museum of Art, New York;
Hugo Kastor Fund, 1962
(plate 194)

74 *
Coast Guard Station, 1929
oil on canvas
29 × 43
Montclair Art Museum, Montclair, New Jersey;
Picture Buying Fund, 1937
(plate 220)

75 *
Railroad Sunset, 1929
oil on canvas
28½ × 47¾
Whitney Museum of American Art, New York;
Bequest of Josephine N. Hopper 70.1170
(plate 382)

76
Tables for Ladies, 1930
oil on canvas
48¼ × 60¼
The Metropolitan Museum of Art, New York;
George A. Hearn Fund, 1931
(plate 329)

77 *
Early Sunday Morning, 1930
oil on canvas
35 × 60
Whitney Museum of American Art, New York;
31.426 (plate 383)

78
The Camel's Hump, 1931
oil on canvas
32¼ × 50⅛
Munson-Williams-Proctor Institute, Utica, New York;
Edward W. Root Bequest
(plate 413)

79
[Cobb's Barns and Distant Houses], c.1931
oil on canvas
28½ × 42
Whitney Museum of American Art, New York;
Bequest of Josephine N. Hopper 70.1206
(plate 411)

80
[Cobb's Barns, South Truro], c.1931
oil on canvas
34 × 50
Whitney Museum of American Art, New York;
Bequest of Josephine N. Hopper 70.1207
(plate 408)

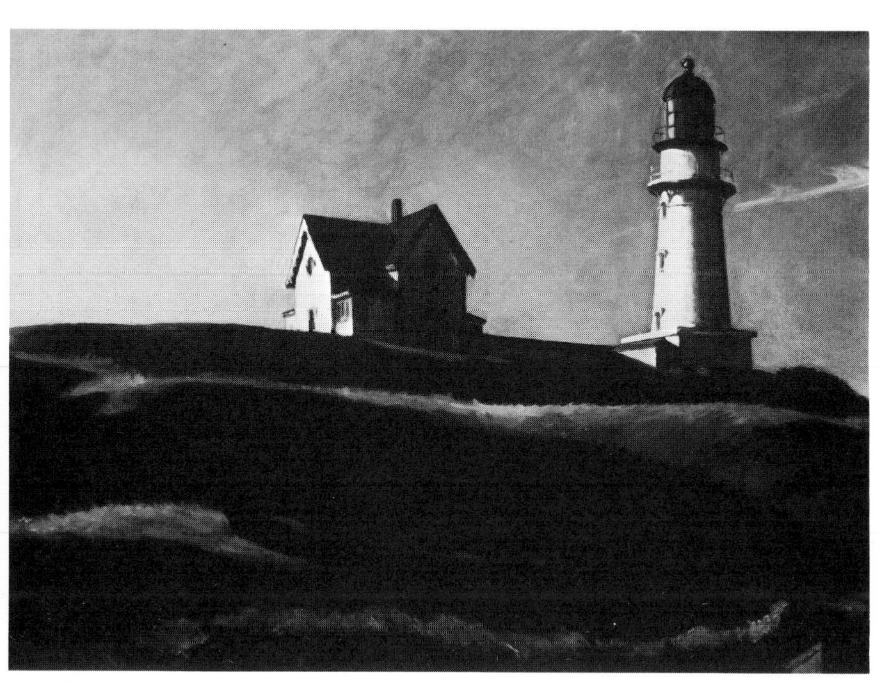

70 · Lighthouse Hill, 1927

81*
Room in New York, 1932
oil on canvas
29 × 36
University of Nebraska Art Galleries, Lincoln;
F.M. Hall Collection
(plate 366)

82
November, Washington Square, 1932 & 1959
oil on canvas
34 × 50
Santa Barbara Museum of Art, California;
Preston Morton Collection
(plate 51)

83
Dawn Before Gettysburg, 1934
oil on canvas
15 × 20
Private Collection, Switzerland
(plate 373)

84
East Wind Over Weehawken, 1934
oil on canvas
24¼ × 50¼
Courtesy of The Pennsylvania Academy of the Fine Arts, Philadelphia;
Collections Fund Purchase, 1952
(plate 248)

85
Macomb's Dam Bridge, 1935
oil on canvas
35 × 60
The Brooklyn Museum, New York;
Bequest of Miss Mary T. Cockeroll
(plate 251)

86
Jo Painting, 1936
oil on canvas
18 × 16
Whitney Museum of American Art, New York;
Bequest of Josephine N. Hopper 70.1171
(plate 44)

87
French Six-Day Bicycle Rider, 1937
oil on canvas
17 × 19
Collection of Mr and Mrs Albert Hackett
(plate 164)

88*
Compartment C, Car 293, 1938
oil on canvas
20 × 18
IBM Corporation, Armonk, New York
(plate 272)

89*
New York Movie, 1939
oil on canvas
32¼ × 40⅛
The Museum of Modern Art, New York;
Given anonymously, 1941
(plate 340)

90*
Bridle Path, 1939
oil on canvas
28 × 42
San Francisco Museum of Modern Art;
Anonymous gift
(plate 254)

91
Pretty Penny, 1939
oil on canvas
29 × 40
Smith College Museum of Art, Northampton, Massachusetts;
Gift of Mrs Charles MacArthur (Helen Hayes LHD '40), 1965
(plate 228)

92
Cape Cod Evening, 1939
oil on canvas
30 × 40
Collection of Mr and Mrs John Hay Whitney
(plate 418)

93*
Gas, 1940
oil on canvas
26¼ × 40¼
The Museum of Modern Art, New York;
Mrs Simon Guggenheim Fund, 1943
(plate 275)

94
Light Battery at Gettysburg, 1940
oil on canvas
18 × 27
Nelson Gallery-Atkins Museum, Kansas City, Missouri;
Gift of the Friends of Art
(plate 375)

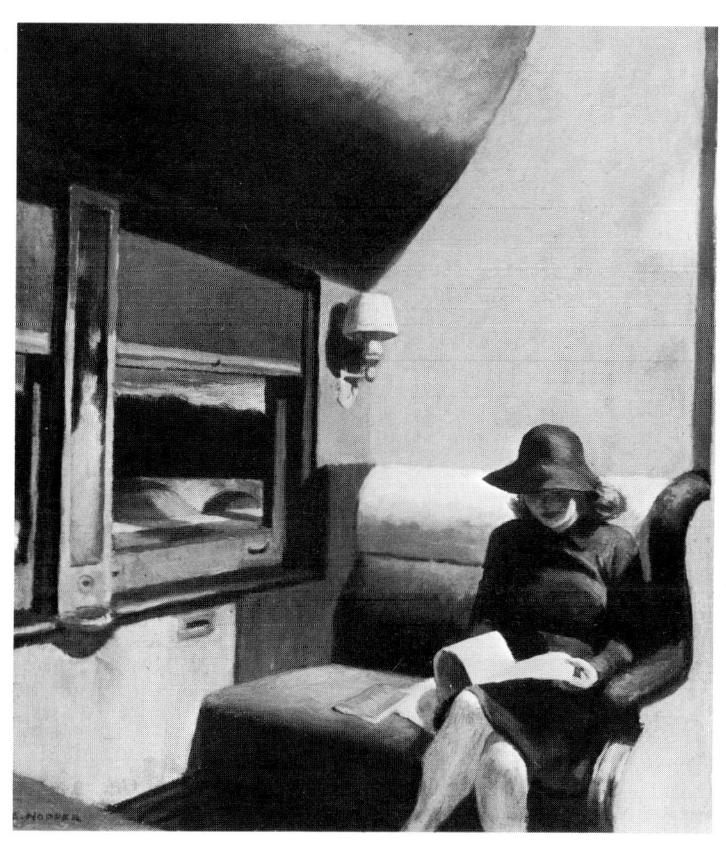

88 · Compartment C, Car 293, 1938

95*
Office at Night, 1940
oil on canvas
22⅛ × 25
Walker Art Center, Minneapolis;
Gift of the T.B. Walker Foundation
(plate 356)

96*
Nighthawks, 1942
oil on canvas
33³⁄₁₆ × 60⅛
The Art Institute of Chicago;
Friends of American Art
(plate 386)

97
Summertime, 1943
oil on canvas
29⅛ × 44
Delaware Art Museum, Wilmington;
Gift of Dora Sexton Brown
(plate 166)

98
Hotel Lobby, 1943
oil on canvas
32½ × 40¾
Indianapolis Museum of Art;
Gift in memory of William Ray Adams
(plate 283)

99
The Martha Mckean of Wellfleet, 1944
oil on canvas
32 × 50
Thyssen-Bornemisza Collection,
Lugano-Castagnola, Switzerland.
(plate 187)

100
August in the City, 1945
oil on canvas
23 × 30
Norton Gallery and School of Art,
West Palm Beach, Florida
(plate 258)

101
Pennsylvania Coal Town, 1947
oil on canvas
28 × 40
The Butler Institute of American Art,
Youngstown, Ohio
(plate 169)

102*
Seven A.M., 1948
oil on canvas
30 × 40
Whitney Museum of American Art, New York,
50.8
(plate 388)

103
High Noon, 1949
oil on canvas
28 × 40
The Dayton Art Institute, Ohio;
Gift of Mr and Mrs Anthony Haswell
(plate 398)

104
Portrait of Orleans, 1950
oil on canvas
26 × 40
Private Collection
(plate 421)

105
First Row Orchestra, 1951
oil on canvas
31⅛ × 40⅛
Hirshhorn Museum and Sculpture Garden,
Smithsonian Institution, Washington, DC
(plate 350)

106
Hotel by a Railroad, 1952
oil on canvas
31¼ × 40⅛
Hirshhorn Museum and Sculpture Garden,
Smithsonian Institution, Washington, DC
(plate 297)

107
Carolina Morning, 1955
oil on canvas
30 × 40
Whitney Museum of American Art, New York
Given in memory of Otto L. Spaeth
by his family 67.13
(plate 322)

108
Hotel Window, 1956
oil on canvas
40 × 55
Thyssen-Bornemisza Collection,
Lugano-Castagnola, Switzerland
(plate 300)

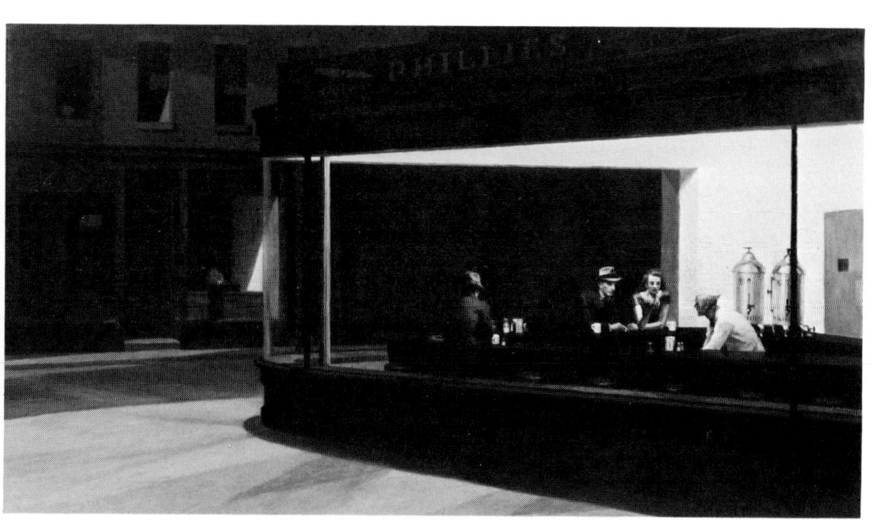

96 · Nighthawks, 1942

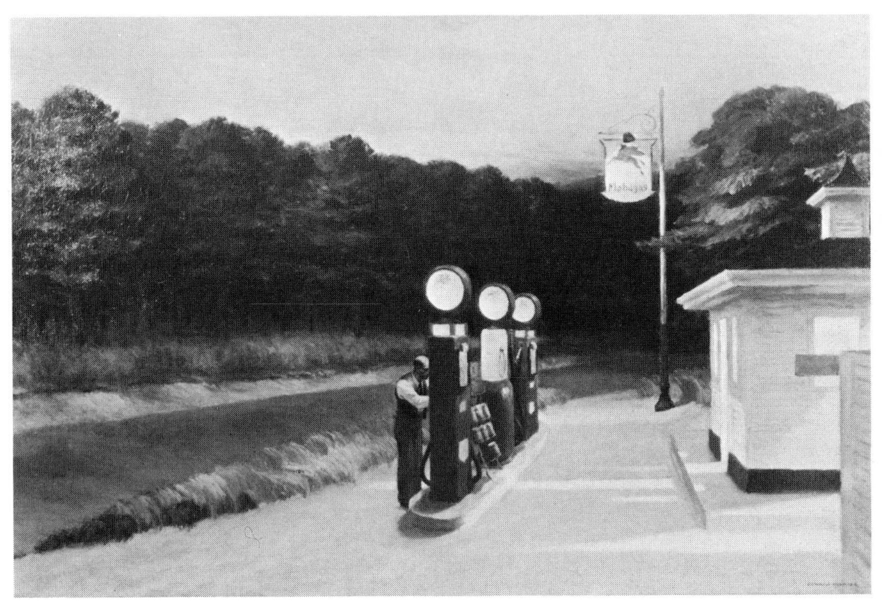

93 · Gas, 1940

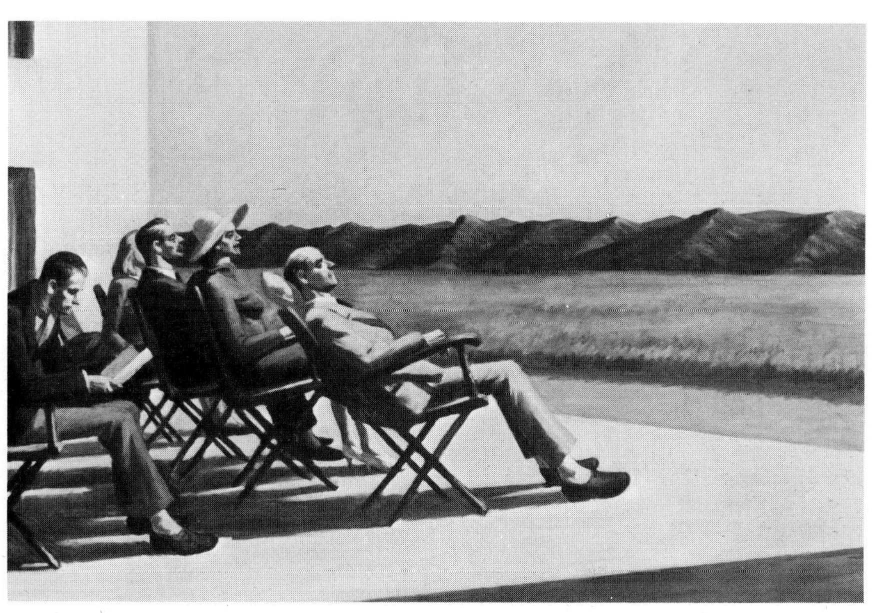

109 · People in the Sun, 1960

109*
People in the Sun, 1960
oil on canvas
40 × 60
National Collection of Fine Arts,
Smithsonian Institution, Washington, DC,
Gift of S.C.Johnson and Son, Inc.
(plate 426)

110
Second Storey Sunlight, 1960
oil on canvas
40 × 50
Whitney Museum of American Art, New York,
Gift of the Friends of the
Whitney Museum of American Art 60.54
(plate 425)

111*
A Woman in the Sun, 1961
oil on canvas
40 × 60
Whitney Museum of American Art, New York,
Partial gift of
Mr and Mrs Albert Hackett in honour of
Edith and Lloyd Goodrich P.18.80
(plate 427)

112
Intermission, 1963
oil on canvas
40 × 60
Collection of Mrs Morris Pelavin
(plate 352)

113
Chair Car, 1965
oil on canvas
40 × 50
Private Collection
(plate 305)

WATERCOLOURS

114
[Hook Mountain, Nyack], c.1899
watercolour on paper
5 × 7
Whitney Museum of American Art, New York, Bequest of Josephine N. Hopper 70.1558.55
(plate 28)

115
[Parisian Woman], 1906-7 or 1909
watercolour on composition board
$11\frac{13}{16} \times 9\frac{7}{16}$
Whitney Museum of American Art, New York, Bequest of Josephine N. Hopper 70.1324
(plate 93)

116
[Parisian Woman Walking], 1906-7 or 1909
watercolour on composition board
$11\frac{13}{16} \times 9\frac{1}{4}$
Whitney Museum of American Art, New York, Bequest of Josephine N. Hopper 70.1323
(plate 94)

117
[Self-Portrait], 1910
watercolour on paper
$18\frac{1}{4} \times 12\frac{1}{4}$
Private Collection
(plate 16)

118
Rock at the Fort, Gloucester, 1924
watercolour on paper
$13\frac{3}{4} \times 19\frac{3}{4}$
Collection of Mr and Mrs Alvin L. Snowiss
(plate 202)

119
House with Bay Window, 1925
watercolour on paper
15 × 20
Private Collection
(plate 213)

120
Skyline, Near Washington Square, 1925
watercolour on paper
$15\frac{1}{16} \times 21\frac{3}{16}$
Munson-Williams-Proctor Institute, Utica, New York;
Edward W. Root Bequest
(plate 238)

121
[St Michael's College, Santa Fe], 1925
watercolour on paper
$13\frac{7}{8} \times 19\frac{15}{16}$
Whitney Museum of American Art, New York; Bequest of Josephine N. Hopper 70.1158
(plate 306)

122
[Jo Sketching at the Beach], 1925-28
watercolour on paper
$13\frac{7}{8} \times 20$
Whitney Museum of American Art, New York; Bequest of Josephine N. Hopper 70.1129
(plate 37)

123
[Reclining Nude], c.1925-30
watercolour on paper
$13\frac{7}{8} \times 19\frac{7}{8}$
Whitney Museum of American Art, New York; Bequest of Josephine N. Hopper 70.1089
(plate 38)

124
Manhattan Bridge and Lily Apartments, 1926
watercolour on paper
$13\frac{1}{2} \times 19\frac{1}{2}$
Collection of Mr and Mrs Joel Harnett
(plate 240)

125
Light at Two Lights, 1927
watercolour on paper
$13\frac{15}{16} \times 19\frac{15}{16}$
Whitney Museum of American Art, New York; Bequest of Josephine N. Hopper 70.1143
(plate 195)

126
Prospect Street, Gloucester, 1928
watercolour on paper
14 × 20
Private Collection
(plate 209)

127
White House with Telephone Poles, c.1930
watercolour on paper
$20 \times 27\frac{7}{8}$
Whitney Museum of American Art, New York; Bequest of Josephine N. Hopper 70.1085

128
High Road, 1931
watercolour on paper
20 × 28
Whitney Museum of American Art, New York; Bequest of Josephine N. Hopper 70.1163
(plate 270)

129
House on Pamet River, 1934
watercolour on paper
20 × 25
Whitney Museum of American Art, New York; 36.20
(plate 225)

130
[**Village Church**], c.1934-35
watercolour on paper
19½ × 25
Whitney Museum of American Art, New York; Bequest of Josephine N. Hopper 70.1086
(plate 226)

131
[**Jo Sketching in the Truro House**], 1934-40
watercolour on paper
13 15/16 × 20
Whitney Museum of American Art, New York; Bequest of Josephine N. Hopper 70.1106
(plate 42)

132
Yawl Riding a Swell, 1935
watercolour on paper
20 1/16 × 28¼
Worcester Art Museum, Worcester, Massachusetts
(plate 183)

133
[**Jo Sleeping**], c.1940-45
watercolour and pencil on illustration board
11 11/16 × 18
Whitney Museum of American Art, New York; Bequest of Josephine N. Hopper 70.1113
(plate 45)

134
El Palacio, 1946
watercolour on paper
20¾ × 28⅝
Whitney Museum of American Art, New York; 50.2
(plate 321)

135
Jo in Wyoming, July 1946
watercolour on paper
13 15/16 × 20
Whitney Museum of American Art, New York; Bequest of Josephine N. Hopper 70.1159
(plate 46)

136
[**Roofs, Saltillo, Mexico**], 1946
watercolour on paper
21 × 29
Whitney Museum of American Art, New York; Bequest of Josephine N. Hopper 70.1162
(plate 320)

DRAWINGS

137
[Restaurant Scene], 1894
pencil on paper
5×8
Whitney Museum of American Art, New York; Bequest of Josephine N. Hopper 70.1561.161
(plate 324)

138
Acrobats, c.1898-99
pencil on paper
$5 \times 7\frac{15}{16}$
Whitney Museum of American Art, New York; Bequest of Josephine N. Hopper 70.1553.21
(plate 331)

139
[Self-Portrait], c.1900
pencil on paper
$10\frac{1}{4} \times 8\frac{1}{4}$
Collection of Mr and Mrs Peter R. Blum
(plate 3)

140
Camp Nyack, 1900
pen and ink on paper
$10 \times 14\frac{1}{2}$
Collection of Dr and Mrs Theodore Leshner, New York
(plate 29)

141
[Self-Portrait], June 5, 1900
conté on paper
14×12
Collection of Mr and Mrs Joel Harnett
(plate 1)

142
[Self-Portrait], 1900
pencil on paper
$5\frac{1}{4} \times 3\frac{3}{4}$
Kennedy Galleries, Inc., New York
(plate 2)

143
Before the Footlights, c.1900
pen and ink on paper
$14\frac{13}{16} \times 5\frac{5}{8}$
Whitney Museum of American Art, New York; Bequest of Josephine N. Hopper 70.1558.82
(plate 334)

144
[Self Portrait and Hand Studies], c.1900
pen and ink on paper
$8\frac{15}{16} \times 5\frac{5}{8}$
Whitney Museum of American Art, New York; Bequest of Josephine N. Hopper 70.1559.21
(plate 4)

145
[Self-Portrait and Hand Studies], c.1900
pen and ink on paper
$7\frac{7}{8} \times 5$
Whitney Museum of American Art, New York; Bequest of Josephine N. Hopper 70.1559.28
(plate 5)

146
[Nude Female Model on Platform], c.1900-1903
charcoal on paper
$18\frac{7}{8} \times 12\frac{1}{8}$
Whitney Museum of American Art, New York; Bequest of Josephine N. Hopper 70.1566.118
(plate 71)

147
[Nude Female Model in Studio], c.1900-1903
charcoal on paper
$12\frac{1}{8} \times 9\frac{1}{2}$
Whitney Museum of American Art, New York; Bequest of Josephine N. Hopper 70.1560.90
(plate 70)

148
[Three Men at an Art Exhibition], 1900-1903
conté on paper
$9\frac{3}{8} \times 6\frac{1}{16}$
Whitney Museum of American Art, New York; Bequest of Josephine N. Hopper 70.1560.51
(plate 69)

149
[Garrett Henry Hopper, The Artist's Father], 1900-1906
conté on paper
$24\frac{1}{4} \times 18\frac{3}{4}$
Whitney Museum of American Art, New York; Bequest of Josephine N. Hopper 70.1549 (recto)
(plate 65)

150
Sketch after Manet's **The Fifer,** 1900-1907
pen and ink on paper
10×7
Whitney Museum of American Art, New York; Bequest of Josephine N. Hopper 70.1560.96
(plate 65)

151
Sketch after Manet's **Olympia,** 1900-1907
pen and ink on paper
8⅞ × 5½
Whitney Museum of American Art, New York; Bequest of Josephine N. Hopper 70.1561.133
(plate 66)

152
Sketch after Regnault's **Salome,** c.1900-1907
pen and ink on paper
10 × 7
Whitney Museum of American Art, New York; Bequest of Josephine N. Hopper 70.1560.98
(plate 63)

153
Sketch after Rodin's **La Vieille Femme,** 1901
pen and ink on paper
8⅞ × 5⅝
Whitney Museum of American Art, New York; Bequest of Josephine N. Hopper 70.1561.106
(plate 62)

154
[Self-Portrait], 1903
charcoal on paper
18½ × 12
National Portrait Gallery, Smithsonian Institution, Washington, DC
(plate 9)

155
Anno Domini XIXCV, 1905
conté on paper
18½ × 24
Whitney Museum of American Art, New York; Bequest of Josephine N. Hopper 70.1532
(plate 336)

156
Cab, Horse and Crowd, 1906-7 or 1909
conté, charcoal and wash with touches of white on paper
18¼ × 14⅞
Whitney Museum of American Art, New York; Bequest of Josephine N. Hopper 70.1436
(plate 88)

157
Dome, 1906-7 or 1909
conté, wash, charcoal, and pencil on paper
21⅜ × 9⅞
Whitney Museum of American Art, New York; Bequest of Josephine N. Hopper 70.1434
(plate 87)

158
[Figures Under a Bridge in Paris], 1906-7 or 1909
conté and wash on illustration board
22⅛ × 15⅛
Whitney Museum of American Art, New York; Bequest of Josephine N. Hopper 70.1339
(plate 90)

159
The Railroad, 1906-7 or 1909
conté, charcoal and wash with touches of white
17¾ × 14⅞
Whitney Museum of American Art, New York; Bequest of Josephine N. Hopper 70.1437
(plate 89)

160
Un Maquereau,
(drawing for painting, **Soir Bleu**), 1914
conté on paper
10 × 8⅜
Whitney Museum of American Art, New York; Bequest of Josephine N. Hopper 70.318
(plate 379)

161
Study for the poster, **Smash the Hun,** 1918
gouache on illustration board
9½ × 6⅜
The Charles Rand Penney Collection
(plate 155)

162
Guy Pène du Bois, 1919
sanguine on paper
21 × 16
Whitney Museum of American Art, New York; Bequest of Josephine N. Hopper 70.907
(plate 34)

163
My Mother, c.1920
sanguine on paper
21 × 15¾
Whitney Museum of American Art, New York; Bequest of Josephine N. Hopper 70.298
(plate 26)

164
[Standing Nude], October 26, 1923
sanguine on paper
19 × 11$^{15}/_{16}$
Whitney Museum of American Art, New York; Bequest of Josephine N. Hopper 70.661
(plate 156)

165
Drawing for painting, **[Stairway]**, c.1925
conté on paper
19¼ × 12⅛
Whitney Museum of American Art, New York;
Bequest of Josephine N. Hopper 70.849
(plate 211)

166
[Reclining Nude on a Couch], 1925-30
charcoal on paper
15⅝ × 18
Whitney Museum of American Art, New York;
Bequest of Josephine N. Hopper 70.296
(plate 39)

167
Light at Two Lights, 1927
conté and charcoal on paper
15 × 22¹⁄₁₆
Whitney Museum of American Art, New York;
Bequest of Josephine N. Hopper 70.683
(plate 192)

168
Drawing for painting,
Macomb's Dam Bridge, 1935
conté on paper
8⅞ × 23½
Whitney Museum of American Art, New York;
Bequest of Josephine N. Hopper 70.440
(plate 252)

169
Drawing for painting,
Macomb's Dam Bridge, 1935
pencil on paper
9¼ × 18¼
Whitney Museum of American Art, New York;
Bequest of Josephine N. Hopper 70.990
(plate 253)

170
[Jo Hopper], 1935-40
conté on paper
15⅛ × 22⅛
Whitney Museum of American Art, New York;
Bequest of Josephine N. Hopper 70.293
(plate 43)

171
Drawing for painting, **Bridle Path,** 1939
conté on paper
22¹⁄₁₆ × 15
Whitney Museum of American Art, New York;
Bequest of Josephine N. Hopper 70.857
(plate 257)

172
Drawing for painting,
Cape Cod Evening, 1939
conté on paper
8½ × 11
Whitney Museum of American Art, New York;
Bequest of Josephine N. Hopper 70.183
(plate 419)

173
Drawing for painting,
Cape Cod Evening, 1939
conté, charcoal and pencil on paper
15 × 22⅛
Whitney Museum of American Art, New York;
Bequest of Josephine N. Hopper 70.338

174
Drawing for painting,
New York Movie; Palace, 1939
conté on paper
8⅞ × 11⅞
Whitney Museum of American Art, New York;
Bequest of Josephine N. Hopper 70.111
(plate 342)

175
Drawing for painting,
New York Movie, 1939
conté on paper
11 × 15
Whitney Museum of American Art, New York;
Bequest of Josephine N. Hopper 70.272
(plate 343)

176
Drawing for painting,
New York Movie, 1939
conté on paper
15⅛ × 7¾
Whitney Museum of American Art, New York;
Bequest of Josephine N. Hopper 70.447
(plate 341)

177
Drawing for painting,
New York Movie, 1939
conté on paper
8½ × 11
Whitney Museum of American Art, New York;
Bequest of Josephine N. Hopper 70.100

178
Drawing for painting,
New York Movie, 1939
conté on paper
11 × 8½
Whitney Museum of American Art, New York;
Bequest of Josephine N. Hopper 70.101

179
Drawing for painting,
New York Movie, 1939
conté on paper
8⅞ × 11⅞
Whitney Museum of American Art, New York;
Bequest of Josephine N. Hopper 70.110

180
Drawing for painting,
New York Movie, 1939
sanguine and pencil on paper
11⅛ × 5
Whitney Museum of American Art, New York;
Bequest of Josephine N. Hopper 70.277

181
Drawing for painting,
New York Movie, 1939
conté on paper
8½ × 11
Whitney Museum of American Art, New York;
Bequest of Josephine N. Hopper 70.94 (verso)

182
Drawing for painting,
New York Movie, 1939
conté on paper
15 × 11
Whitney Museum of American Art, New York;
Bequest of Josephine N. Hopper 70.452

183
Drawing for painting,
New York Movie, 1939
conté on paper
11 × 8½
Whitney Museum of American Art, New York;
Bequest of Josephine N. Hopper 70.96

184
Drawing for painting,
New York Movie, 1939
conté on paper
14 15/16 × 11⅛
Whitney Museum of American Art, New York;
Bequest of Josephine N. Hopper 70.455

185
Drawing for painting,
Pretty Penny, 1939
conté on paper
10½ × 16
Whitney Museum of American Art, New York;
Bequest of Josephine N. Hopper 70.681
(plate 230)

186
Drawing for painting,
Gas, 1940
conté and charcoal with touches of
white paint on paper
15 × 22⅛
Whitney Museum of American Art, New York;
Bequest of Josephine N. Hopper 70.349
(plate 277)

187
Drawing for painting,
Office at Night, 1940
conté on paper
8½ × 11
Whitney Museum of American Art, New York;
Bequest of Josephine N. Hopper 70.168
(plate 357)

188
Drawing for painting,
Office at Night, 1940
conté and charcoal with touches of
white paint on paper
15 × 19⅝
Whitney Museum of American Art, New York;
Bequest of Josephine N. Hopper 70.340
(plate 359)

189
Drawing for painting,
Office at Night, 1940
conté on paper
8½ × 11
Whitney Museum of American Art, New York;
Bequest of Josephine N. Hopper 70.166 (verso)

190
Drawing for painting,
Office at Night, 1940
conté on paper
8½ × 11
Whitney Museum of American Art, New York
Bequest of Josephine N. Hopper 70.167

191
Drawing for painting,
Office at Night, 1940
conté on paper
8½ × 11
Whitney Museum of American Art, New York
Bequest of Josephine N. Hopper 70.169

192
Drawing for painting,
Nighthawks, 1942
conté on paper
7¾ × 14
Collection of Mr and Mrs Peter R. Blum
(plate 387)

193
Drawing for painting,
Nighthawks, 1942
conté on paper
$7\frac{1}{4} \times 4\frac{1}{2}$
Whitney Museum of American Art, New York;
Bequest of Josephine N. Hopper 70.189

194
Drawing for painting,
Nighthawks, 1942
conté on paper
$7\frac{1}{4} \times 4\frac{1}{2}$
Whitney Museum of American Art, New York;
Bequest of Josephine N. Hopper 70.190

195
Drawing for painting,
Nighthawks, 1942
conté on paper
$4\frac{1}{2} \times 7\frac{1}{4}$
Whitney Museum of American Art, New York;
Bequest of Josephine N. Hopper 70.192

196
Drawing for painting,
Nighthawks, 1942
conté on paper
$8\frac{1}{2} \times 11$
Whitney Museum of American Art, New York;
Bequest of Josephine N. Hopper 70.193

197
Drawing for painting,
Nighthawks, 1942
conté on paper
$8\frac{1}{2} \times 11$
Whitney Museum of American Art, New York;
Bequest of Josephine N. Hopper 70.195

198
Drawing for painting,
Nighthawks, 1942
conté on paper
$11\frac{7}{8} \times 8\frac{7}{8}$
Whitney Museum of American Art, New York;
Bequest of Josephine N. Hopper 70.254

199
Drawing for painting,
Nighthawks, 1942
conté on paper
$15\frac{1}{8} \times 11\frac{1}{16}$
Whitney Museum of American Art, New York;
Bequest of Josephine N. Hopper 70.256

200
Drawing for painting,
Hotel Lobby, 1943
conté and pencil on paper
$8\frac{1}{2} \times 11$
Whitney Museum of American Art, New York;
Bequest of Josephine N. Hopper 70.116
(plate 285)

201
Drawing for painting,
Hotel Lobby, 1943
conté on paper
$8\frac{1}{2} \times 11$
Whitney Museum of American Art, New York;
Bequest of Josephine N. Hopper 70.117
(plate 284)

202
Drawing for painting,
Hotel Lobby, 1943
conté on paper
15×22
Whitney Museum of American Art, New York;
Bequest of Josephine N. Hopper 70.839
(plate 287)

203
Drawing for painting,
Hotel Lobby, 1943
conté on paper
$15 \times 22\frac{1}{8}$
Whitney Museum of American Art, New York;
Bequest of Josephine N. Hopper 70.996
(plate 286)

204
Drawing for painting,
Summertime, 1943
conté on paper
$8\frac{1}{2} \times 11$
Whitney Museum of American Art, New York;
Bequest of Josephine N. Hopper 70.458
(plate 168)

205
[Self-Portrait], 1945
conté on paper
$22\frac{1}{8} \times 15$
Whitney Museum of American Art, New York;
Bequest of Josephine N. Hopper 70.336
(plate 21)

206
[Jo Hopper], 1945-50
charcoal on paper
$18 \times 15\frac{1}{2}$
Whitney Museum of American Art, New York;
Bequest of Josephine N. Hopper 70.288
(plate 48)

207
Drawing for painting,
Pennsylvania Coal Town, 1947
conté and pencil on paper
11⅛ × 15
Whitney Museum of American Art, New York;
Bequest of Josephine N. Hopper 70.229
(plate 170)

208
Drawing for painting,
First Row Orchestra, 1951
conté on paper
17 1/16 × 20 7/16
Whitney Museum of American Art, New York;
Bequest of Josephine N. Hopper 70.841
(plate 351)

209
Drawing for painting,
Hotel by a Railroad, 1952
conté on paper
12 × 19
Whitney Museum of American Art, New York;
Bequest of Josephine N. Hopper 70.427
(plate 298)

Biographical notes

These notes are drawn from the chronology in *Edward Hopper: The Art and the Artist* by Gail Levin.

1882 Born in Nyack, New York

1899-1900 Studied illustration in New York at a commercial art school.

1900-1906 Studied illustration and painting at the New York School of Art where his fellow students included Gifford Beal, George Bellows, Patrick Henry Bruce, Glenn O. Coleman, Guy Pène du Bois and Rockwell Kent. His painting teachers were Robert Henri, William Merritt Chase and Kenneth Hayes Miller.

1906 Went to Paris in October where he stayed until June of the following year and renewed his friendship with Patrick Henry Bruce.

1907 Visited London, Amsterdam, Haarlem, Berlin and Brussels in July before returning to New York in August where he worked as a commercial artist.

1909 Further stay in Paris between March and July.

1910 Last visit to Paris in May and June, including a journey to Madrid and Toledo. On his return to New York he worked in commercial art and illustration, painting in his free time.

1913 Exhibited one oil painting in the Armory Show (*Sailing* which sold for 250 dollars, his last sale of a painting for ten years).
Moved to 3 Washington Square North where he lived until his death.

1914 Painted during the summer in Ogunquit, Maine.

1915 Took up etching. Exhibited *Soir Bleu* and *New York Corner* in February at the MacDowell Club of New York. Second summer in Ogunquit, Maine.

1916-1919 Painted during the summer on Monhegan Island, Maine.

1919 His poster *Smash the Hun* won an award and was exhibited with those of other contestants in the windows of Gimbel's department store, New York.

1920 First one-man exhibition in the Whitney Studio Club.

1923	Summer in Gloucester, Massachusetts. Stopped etching and began to paint watercolours more regularly. Exhibited six watercolours in a group show at the Brooklyn Museum in the autumn. The museum purchased *The Mansard Roof* for 100 dollars.
1924	Married Josephine Nivison in July. Summer in Gloucester, Mass. One-Man exhibition of watercolours at the Frank K.M. Rehn Gallery, New York. 16 watercolours were sold and Hopper was able to give up his work as a commercial artist.
1925	Visited Colorado and New Mexico. Henceforward he travelled extensively in the United States and Mexico, making many of his journeys by car.
1932	Exhibited in the first Whitney Museum of American Art Biennial.
1933	Retrospective exhibition at the Museum of Modern Art, New York. Purchased land at South Truro.
1934	Built summer house and studio at South Truro.
1935	Awarded Temple Gold Medal, Pennsylvania Academy of the Fine Arts.
1937	Awarded first W.A. Clark Prize and Corcoran Gold Medal, Corcoran Gallery of Art, Washington.
1942	Awarded Ada S. Garrett Prize, The Art Institute of Chicago.
1943	First trip to Mexico, by train.
1945	Elected member of the National Institute of Arts and Letters.
1950	Retrospective exhibition at the Whitney Museum of American Art. This exhibition also shown in Boston and Detroit.
1952	Represented the United States at the Venice Biennale.
1953	On the editorial committee of the pamphlet *Reality* which promoted the cause of representational painting.
1955	Gold Medal for Painting from the American Academy of Arts and Letters.
1956	Awarded Huntington Hartford Foundation fellowship.
1960	Received the Annual Award of *Art in America.*
1962	Complete graphic work exhibited at the Philadelphia Museum of Art and publication of catalogue raisonné.
1964	Retrospective at the Whitney Museum of American Art, also shown in Chicago, Detroit and St Louis.

965 Last painting *Two Comedians.*

967 Died in New York on May 15.

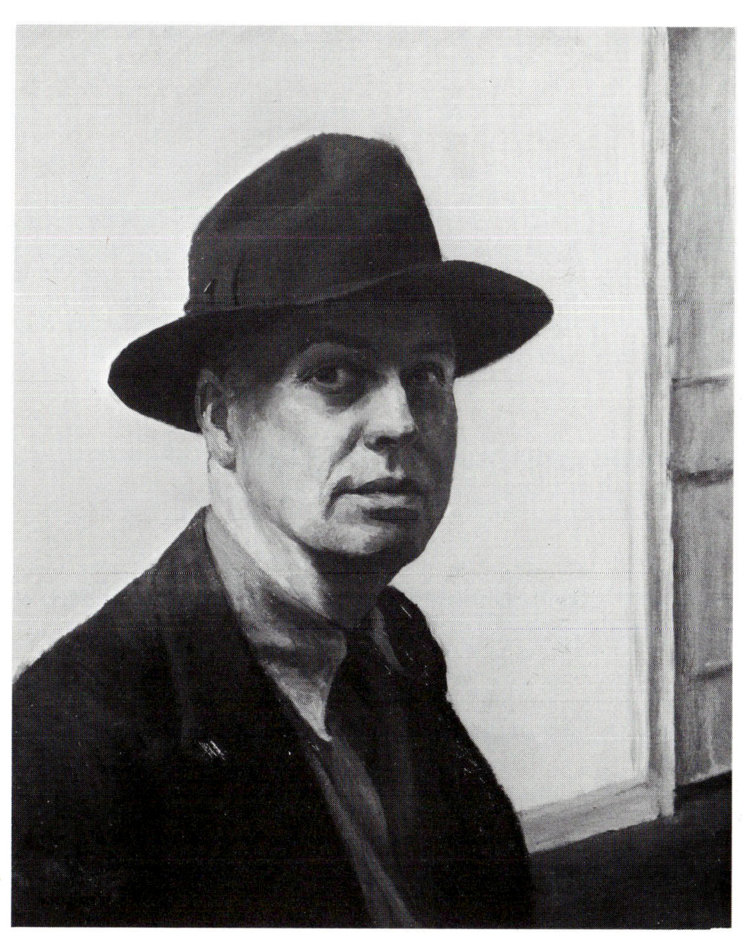

68 · Self-Portrait, 1925-30

Short bibliography

Note: a more complete bibliography is included in Gail Levin's monograph *Edward Hopper: The Art and the Artist* details of which are given below.

Barr, Alfred H., Jr.
Edward Hopper: Retrospective Exhibition.
New York: The Museum of Modern Art, 1933

Brown, Milton W.
American Painting from the Armory Show to the Depression.
Princeton, New Jersey: Princeton University Press, 1955.

Goodrich, Lloyd.
Edward Hopper.
Harmondsworth, England: Penguin Books, 1949.

Goodrich, Lloyd.
Edward Hopper Retrospective Exhibition.
New York: Whitney Museum of American Art, 1950

Goodrich, Lloyd.
Edward Hopper. Exhibition Catalogue.
New York: Whitney Museum of American Art, 1964.

Goodrich, Lloyd.
Edward Hopper.
New York: Harry N. Abrahams, 1971.

Goodrich, Lloyd.
Edward Hopper: Selections from the Hopper Bequest to the Whitney Museum of American Art.
New York: Whitney Museum of American Art, 1971.

Hopper, Edward.
'Books' (review of Malcolm C. Salaman, *Fine Prints of the Year, 1925*).
The Arts, 9 (March 1926). pp. 172-74.

Hopper, Edward.
'John Sloan and the Philadelphians.'
The Arts, 11 (April 1927). pp. 168-78.

Hopper, Edward.
'Books' (review of Vernon Blake, *The Art and Craft of Drawing*).
The Arts, 11 (June 1927), pp. 333-34.

Hopper, Edward.
'Charles Burchfield: American.'
The Arts, 14 (July 1928). pp. 5-12.

Hopper, Edward.
'Edward Hopper Objects' (letter to Nathaniel Pousette-Dart).
The Art of Today, 6 (February 1935), p.11.

Hopper, Edward.
'Statements by Four Artists.'
Reality, 1 (Spring 1953), p.8

Hopper, Edward.
Collected correspondence.
Whitney Museum of American Art, New York.

Levin, Gail.
Edward Hopper as Illustrator.
New York: W.W. Norton & Company in association with the Whitney Museum of American Art, 1979.

Levin, Gail.
Edward Hopper: The Complete Prints.
New York: W.W. Norton & Company in association with the Whitney Museum of American Art, 1979.

Levin, Gail.
Edward Hopper: The Art and The Artist.
New York: W.W. Norton & Company in association with the Whitney Museum of American Art, 1980.

FILM

Edward Hopper, a Four Corner film by Ron Peck has been commissioned by the Arts Council and will be shown at the Hayward Gallery during the exhibition.

A list of Arts Council publications, including all exhibition catalogues in print, can be obtained from the Publications Officer, Arts Council of Great Britain, 105 Piccadilly, London W1V 0AU.